PENGUIN HANDBOOKS
THE ARK RESTAURANT COOKBOOK

Nanci Main, a San Francisco native, and Jimella Lucas, originally from southern Oregon, have owned The Ark Restaurant in Nahcotta, Washington, since 1981. Ms. Main manages the service in the restaurant and bakes the desserts and breads for which the restaurant is well known. She is an award-winning graduate of the Culinary Arts program at Seattle Community College and has worked previously as a chef in the Seattle area. Ms. Lucas's special understanding of cooking with fish comes from her wide range of experience as a chef as well as time spent working on commercial fishing boats. She and Ms. Main are currently at work on a new book.

The *Ark*

RESTAURANT COOKBOOK

CUISINE
of the Pacific Northwest

Jimella Lucas & Nanci Main

PENGUIN BOOKS

PENGUIN BOOKS

Viking Penguin Inc., 40 West 23rd Street, New York, New York 10010, U.S.A.
Penguin Books Ltd, Harmondsworth, Middlesex, England
Penguin Books Australia Ltd, Ringwood, Victoria, Australia
Penguin Books Canada Limited, 2801 John Street, Markham, Ontario, Canada L3R 1B4
Penguin Books (N.Z.) Ltd, 182–190 Wairau Road, Auckland 10, New Zealand

First published in the United States of America by
Ladysmith Limited Publishing Company 1983
Published in Penguin Books 1985

LIBRARY OF CONGRESS CATALOGING IN PUBLICATION DATA
Lucas, Jimella.
The Ark Restaurant cookbook.
Reprint. Originally published: The Ark.
St. Louis, Mo.: Ladysmith, © 1983.
Includes index.
1. Ark Restaurant (Nahcotta, Wash.).
2. Cookery, American—Northwest, Pacific.
I. Main, Nanci.   II. Title.
TX945.5.A75L83   1985   641.5   85-12183
ISBN 0 14 046.731 9

Editing, introductions, vignettes: Dick Friedrich, Angela Harris,
Elisabeth McPherson, Michael J. Salevouris
Art direction: Beverly Alden Bishop
Book design: Wiseman Design
Photo credits:
Pages 49 & 127 — Michael J. Salevouris; pages 7, 17, 29, 67, 107, 163, & 189 —
Beverly Alden Bishop

Printed in the United States of America by
R. R. Donnelley & Sons Company, Harrisonburg, Virginia
Set in Cheltenham

TABLE OF CONTENTS

Introduction

CHEF'S INTRODUCTION

*This book is
dedicated to our partner-
ship of creating and
sharing simply good food.*

When you pull up in front of THE ARK,
you see a kind of ordinary, blue, one-story
building on the shore of Willapa Bay. The
large windows facing the water probably tell
you that the person who designed the building
wanted you to be able to watch the herons
fish and the tides move, the gulls soar and the
clouds roll.

On the shore side of the building sit three
abandoned boats — a couple of fishing boats
and a dinghy, looking for all the world as
though the bay got angry one night and washed them up there.

When you look out on the water after
dark, you see an almost eerie scene — the
hallogen lights pointed on the bay shore wash
a shimmering layer of whiteness over the
water and the bay grass.

Perhaps the most remarkable sight is the
two-story pile of oyster shells — silent but elo-
quent testimony to tens of thousands of
oysters served over the years.

But the real point of the restaurant is
neither its architecture nor its landscaping.
The real focus of THE ARK is the magical moment when we serve our food to our guest.

This is what THE ARK is about. For years, our lives pointed toward this moment, towards this restaurant; long hours fishing commercially, waiting tables at a dozen different restaurants throughout the United States, school, apprenticeships, cafe work, restaurant work, our catering business, then our first restaurant, the Shelburne. All this and more focus on each meal we serve; when you sit down to eat at THE ARK, what you taste comes from our years of preparation, as well as our dedication to certain ideals.

We insist on the finest fresh fruits, vegetables, meats, poultry and seafoods. It is that concern for quality and the love we have for the Pacific Northwest that lead us to use primarily local products. Where else outside our locale can you find Willapa Bay Oysters, Oregon Blue Cheese, Oregon strawberries, Washington wild blackberries, Oregon Veal, Columbia River salmon and sturgeon? We have them all; we serve them fresh. And we want you to look out our windows and see the sources of our bounty.

We bring these unique ingredients to the table prepared uniquely because we work from our sense to yours. Just as a painter chooses colors and shapes and lines to appeal to his or her own eye and the eye of the beholder. Just as the composer arranges notes and rhythms and instruments to please musicians and listener. Just as any other kind of artist, we think of our raw material — the food we have access to. Then we let those flavors, aromas and colors speak to us. We let the flavors, the textures lead us. We express ourselves with our recipes; we tell you who we are. We are no fans of slavishly followed recipes. We experiment; we want you to do the same.

Recipes can be traps: they can strangle chefs in their formula clutches. We want rather to share our enthusiasm, our excitement with you. To involve you in the exhileration that comes with crashing out of the false limits. Rules say, "This way and no other." We say — no. Let your ingredients speak to you with their special and unique qualities, colors, textures. Follow the flavors; fulfill your senses. Experience the liberty of creating with us. We want this book to capture the spirit of THE ARK — the sense of personal involvement in the preparation of food.

Obviously, plants, animals — all living things on this planet use food. Some even show preferences, choosing some foods over others. But only humans combine and prepare their foods to attract and satisfy their aesthetic sense: only humans have made an art of their food. We want you to celebrate with us exuberantly and lovingly.

Nancei

Junelle

JAMES BEARD ON THE ARK

Years ago — over 60 — we had a home
on the Oregon coast just below Astoria, in
Gearhart, and I knew the whole coast down to
Newport, Tillamook, Depoe Bay and even further south. I was also acquainted with the
Washington side, through Chinook, Ilwaco,
Long Beach, Ocean Park and on to Oysterville
and Grays Harbor. During my long lifetime,
which has spanned eight decades, there has
never been a restaurant that glorified the great
gifts from the sea, nor the fine vegetables, or
the wild mushrooms, or the small fruits or the
game. All of this bounty was exclusively for
those who wanted to search it out for themselves and cook it in their homes. When I was
in the Northwest about three years ago I was
told that all that had changed. I was told of a
restaurant in a small hotel which had been a
popular hotel in the summer. The Shelburne
was a new development and it really had the
makings of a heralded dining spot specializing
in the foods from the sea; the native clams,
the Dungeness crab, the sweetwater crayfish,
the mussels, the perch and the many types of
flounder and sole and the lordly sturgeon and
the roe sieved into caviar and the roe of the
salmon, the cheeks of the salmon and the
salmon itself — all these incredible and fresh

fish and shellfish — this bounty which, to a great extent, had been grossly neglected. I vaguely remember one restaurant in Seaside which served fish but only fried salmon or fried clams or fried cracked crab. No attempt was made to show the contrasting textures and flavors of all the dishes served along the coast.

In addition, there were the oysters; the Olympias, the Shoalwater bay oysters, all splendidly fresh. Few people took advantage of them. I knew some who were in the oyster business and had sacks of them transported across the bay or up to Portland but never paid any attention to them in most restaurants. It was tragic. Well, I went to the Shelburne, at the suggestion of some friends, where Jimella Lucas and Nanci Main were ensconced for the first period of their professional lives, with some misgivings. I had doubts that anyone was giving the gifts from the sea its due and I was mistaken! During the first meal there I felt — and hoped — that this was something that we had all waited for for many years. I tried, that first summer, to blow the trumpet and wave the banners around through Gearhart and Seaside and Cannon Beach. I think I enlisted a small army of co-boosters who spread the word much further. The restaurant thrived. There was new imagination. There was new creativity. There was variety and there was goodness. Jimella Lucas is a person who was schooled in the lore of fish, who has handled fish, and who has known cooking fish. She has taste. She has imagination and, she is able to create new and exciting menus with what she has at hand. Nanci Main is a person with menu ability, who has the gift of charming the ovens as a pastry cook. She has imagination. She complements Jimella's creativity with her own. It is no wonder that this restaurant was successful from the very start because it served a public that had grown much more palate-conscious than most of the public which patronized the beach resorts in the years before. People have learned more about cooking, they have learned more about eating. They are more discerning. This offered them an opportunity to revel in some of the goodies, not only the fish but the chanterelle and the other wild mushrooms and the vegetables that abound in the sandy soil and have a quality that one seldom finds anywhere else.

The early restaurant had its rather picturesque, Victorian charm in the dining room and it was reminiscent of a fantastic atmosphere. The restaurant flourished and Jimella and Nanci were faced with expansion. They discovered a huge restaurant built over the

water near Oysterville, which had been called
THE ARK and had oyster plants across the
road from it and oyster beds around it. As a
result they dared to move in and it has been a
success. It has given them a chance for development. It's given them a chance to do many
different dishes and to create new ideas and to
further their success. That they have caught
on with the public is an established fact. People are taken with it. They like it. They want
to reserve places not only for summer but
winter as well. They celebrate most of the
holidays in seasonal fashion. The restaurant attracts many beach addicts. Some just
drive in for dinner and go back to Portland,
Olympia, Seattle or Tacoma. People come
from as far as Newport. It's definitely a success
story and it stands to reason that Jimella and
Nanci fancied the furtherance of their dreams
and theories. It is not surprising, then, that
they have incorporated these feelings in a
book. It is a reflection of their personalities, of
their ideas about food, of their ways of serving
it, and chance for those who have eaten there
to recreate some of the recipes which they
have enjoyed at THE ARK, not just run of the
mill recipes, but new ways with fish, new
ways with shell fish and new ideas. There are
some of Nanci's sweets and hints about
menus. It is truly a regional book!

James Beard
May, 1983

The Region, The Ark

THE REGION, THE ARK

Ten miles south of the Ark Restaurant, in Long Beach, an unpretentious monument marks the westernmost point of the famous Lewis and Clark expedition. The 1804-1806 expedition has long been considered one of the signal events in the history of the region, and rightly so. But when Meriwether Lewis, William Clark and their "Corps of Discovery" first spied the storm-tossed Pacific they were certainly not the first whites to visit the area. In their **Journals** the explorers mention their encounter with a Clatsop "Indian" who had light skin, freckles and "long dusky red hair." Equally curious were the Indians who already knew some English words like "musquit, powder,...file [and] damned rascal." Clearly, whites were hardly strangers to the Pacific coast and the Columbia basin.

In fact, for the previous two centuries European traders, adventurers, and explorers paid regular visits. They came to seek the fabled Northwest Passage and the land rich in gold, silver and pearls described in the fabulous and exaggerated travel-tales of Juan de Fuca. They came to trade for the prized pelts of the sea otter. They came to claim more territories for the monarchs they served. Sir Francis Drake reached north Pacific waters in 1579. Later visitors included Captain James Cook (1778), Captain George Vancouver and Lieutenant Peter Puget (1792), and the American, Robert Gray, who discovered, in 1792, the mouth of the river that now bears the name of his ship — the Columbia.

For all that, before the nineteenth century the impact of white people on the Northwest was minimal. For literally thousands of years before the coming of Europeans, the land was inhabited by the Indians. An abundance of food and a mild climate (winters are colder in Washington , D. C., than in Juneau, Alaska) allowed the Indian tribes of the Pacific Northwest to develop one of the most complex and sophisticated hunting and gathering cultures the world has ever known.

The shores of Willapa Bay and the mouth of the Columbia River were home to the Chinook tribe, the trading entrepreneurs among the Northwest Indians. Long before the earliest whites arrived, the Chinooks held annual trade fairs at The Dalles which attracted goods from as far away as Alaska and the Great Plains. The Chinook language became the basis for a trade jargon used the length of the river — a language that later incorporated a number of European words and phrases. The word "chinook" survives today as an equatorial trade wind whose warmth can melt a heavy fall of snow between night and morning. And for those who fish, those who cook fish, and those who eat it a "chinook" means the royalty of salmon.

Lewis and Clark (in the words of William Goetzmann) "succeeded in making the West itself an object of desire." In so doing they heralded the destruction of Indian culture and the gradual conquest of the region by a steady stream of pioneer settlers.

On Willapa Bay one of the earliest settlements was Oysterville, first settled in 1854. Oysterville quickly grew to more than five hundred residents and at least five saloons catering to those who worked the oyster beds, the reason for the town's existence. The town boasted the County Seat until 1893 when eighty-five men from South Bend descended on the courthouse and, in spite of the auditor's valiant defense and a spirited battle with chair legs, made off with all the county records and with them the county government.

In the early years life in Oysterville was riotous and gay. In contrast, Ocean Park had more sedate beginnings. About 1884, ten laymen acquired 140 acres of land and formed the Methodist Camp Meeting Association. The idea was to combine a summer resort with a revival meeting. The camp meetings lasted for some years and then faded away. As one worshipper said, "The plan of adjusting hours of services to fit the bathing tides did not add to the spiritual power of gatherings."

The town of Nahcotta (the home of The Ark) was created about 1889 with the coming of the new narrow gauge railroad. Before the line was finished, two of the railroad's major stockholders quarreled. B. A. Seaborg bought land on one side of the track and established a town called Sealand and built a hotel. Lewis Loomis started a town on the other side, called Nahcotta, and built his own hotel. A wharf was built into the bay so lumber could be loaded on the trains; stores opened; houses were built. Then about twenty years after Nahcotta was founded, one of the hotels caught fire and the town was reduced to ashes. The town maintained a store and a post office well into this century, its enormous heap of oyster shells, its oyster processing plant, and, of course, The Ark Restaurant.

Early in the 1950's a small restaurant called "The Ark" opened in Nahcotta, across the road from the oyster cannery. Its proprietor, Lucille Wilson, was no outlander, hoping to make a fortune from the natives and the tourists. Mrs. Wilson was the third generation to be born in Oysterville — her grandmother in 1861, her mother in 1893 — and the mother of her husband Lew had been born in the same town in 1888. The new restaurant flourished. Oysters, the principal menu item, weren't days or weeks old; it was only hours since they had been alive in the bay. A special feature was an oyster feed: all the fried oysters you could eat, for a price set before you began. One regular summer visitor remembers those fried oysters for Sunday breakfast as the most satisfying meals she ever ate.

The old Ark burned in 1971, and although it was rebuilt, larger and more modern, with even bigger windows directly above the tideflats of the bay, for Lucille Wilson it wasn't the same. She sold out the next year.

In 1981, Jimella Lucas and Nanci Main who had operated a restaurant further south on the peninsula bought The Ark. Their special gifts with seafood and local produce have brought them a large following of loyal diners from the peninsula as well as those who regularly travel from Portland and Seattle.

Their reputation has brought them visits from food editors across the country and from not a few food lovers who will travel from San Francisco, St. Louis, New York and Miami for a fine meal.

Both Lucas and Main trained extensively in restaurants, schools, and clubs in the Pacific Northwest. Lucas' background includes work in commercial fishing, invaluable training for someone who loves creating dishes from the bounty of the sea. Main is a prize winning dessert chef who also produces breads and muffins to complement every meal.

Since Lucas and Main bought THE ARK "all the oysters you can eat" still appears on the menu but so does much more to delight the diner.

Michael J. Salevouris
Elisabeth McPherson

Using Your Ark Cookbook

Congratulations. You have one of the finest cookbooks available today. Whether you bought it for yourself or someone gave it to you as a gift, you have happy times ahead preparing some of the most exquisite meals ever served from your kitchen.

The items you find here come from one of the finest "informal" gourmet restaurants in the country, yet the recipes, prepared by Chefs Nanci Main (desserts and breads mostly) and Jimella Lucas (entrees etc.), work so easily that your eating life will change dramatically.

Sound like a preposterous claim? Perhaps. But once you have had your first taste of Chicken and Scallops with Tarragon, once you have served your first meal using the Barbeque Sauce, once you have tasted the astonishing light — rich Swedish Cream — you will understand.

Following these hints regarding the use of THE ARK cookbook should make everything both smooth and simple as well as elegant.

The classical gourmet style of the recipes necessitates reading each recipe thoroughly and completely ahead of time. Know the steps: know the order you need to follow. A couple extra minutes reading and planning will save later inconveniences.

You'll notice an occasional asterisk next to an ingredient or a step in the recipe. That mark tells you that you'll find a tip at the end of the recipe regarding that specific ingredient or step. Again: reading the whole recipe thoroughly from start to finish will add immensely to your enjoyment in preparing and eating from THE ARK cookbook.

Use the freshest and highest quality ingredients available, including fresh ground pepper, fresh herbs as well as fresh seafood, fruits and vegetables. Always have the ingredients chopped, sliced, measured before starting.

A few of the recipes make large quantities; Chef Lucas has developed her specialities for her restaurant. The Bouillabaisse, for example, makes quite a bit, but making a large amount makes possible the delicate balance of a number of subtle flavors. Make the quantity called for and freeze what you don't eat; that way you always have the royalty of seafood dishes available — simply add your own catches of the day.

Keep your freezer well-stocked with bouillabaisse, tomato sauce, pesto, cake for chocolate cranberry tortes, breads and the like. If you prepare ahead, you'll never be stuck for an elegant meal.

Keep the following in your refrigerator: clarified butter, roux, seasoned bread crumbs.

To clarify butter, melt it in a pitcher. Let it settle; remove the fat. The oil remaining will tolerate the high temperatures needed to saute.

For **roux,** melt ½ **c butter** in a saucepan until it is totally rendered and starts to bubble. Add ¾ **c flour** slowly and cook on low heat 5 to 10 minutes, stirring constantly. The temperature is important here, in order to have matured roux; don't add flour before the butter is bubbling. Cover in air tight container and refrigerate what you don't use for future recipes.

For **seasoned bread crumbs** combine **1½ slices stale bread, 2 bunches parsley, ½ clove garlic, 1 T parmesan, grated, dash tabasco,** in food processor and process until finely ground.

Do not use what grocery stores like to call "cooking wine;" use wine of at least the same quality that you intend to drink. When a recipe calls for sherry, use high quality dry sherry; when it calls for sauterne, use drinking sauterne or a good dry vermouth.

Now then, you no doubt have noticed some of the very special features of this book; perhaps you chose it for one or more of them. The pictures and the pieces about and from the region do not fit here as extraneous decoration any more than the sauce in Salmon Lucas or the genache in Caramelo. Rather they form integral parts of the whole cooking and eating experience. The extensive use of cranberries, for example, reflects the large cranberry bogs just down the road. The oysters, the salmon, the sturgeon, the crabs all come to THE ARK right from neighboring waters. (In fact, some of those waters butt right up against THE ARK.) Chefs Lucas and Main have deep commitments to the foods from their locales. They don't simply use the foods; they caress them, they live them. The preparations here grow from Chefs Main and Lucas much as the foods grow on the land and in the water.

The book provides you with a sense of THE ARK's setting — both historical and geographical. We have here not just a location, not just another good cookbook, but a way of life, a special connection to the earth and ocean, an attitude toward the bounty coming from both.

We hope that you will find cooking and eating from this book to be the next best thing to being at THE ARK. Skol. Salute.

Dick Friedrich
Angela Harris
Editors

Appetizers

A Century Of Oysters

When white people first saw Willapa Bay in the nineteenth century it was nothing but a huge oyster bed. Chinook Indians had been harvesting, drying, and eating the oysters for centuries without noticably diminishing the supply. Surely they would last forever. But in less than forty years they were gone. Between 1851, when Charles Russell sent the first load of oysters to San Francisco by steamship, and 1889, when the last shipment left, the oysters disappeared.

The native oysters were delicate and small, not much larger than a big man's thumb. They were enormously popular in San Francisco, where a bushel sold for seven dollars, and they may have provided more gold for the oystermen in Oysterville and the rival Bruceport than hunting gold did for the goldseekers who bought them. About 50,000 baskets a year were shipped out of the bay.

The problem was that no shells were put back in the bay to act as clutch to which the young oysters could attach themselves. Between 1890 and 1929, carloads of eastern oyster seed were brought in, but the same cycle was repeated. About 1931 the spat of larger Pacific oysters was brought in from Japan. It was in the middle of the depression and "oyster wars" ensued; a quart of shucked oysters could be bought in Portland for as little as 25¢.

But the oystermen had learned. Now the shells are pierced, hung on wires, and placed where they can attract the tiny eggs. After a winter of careful attention, the shells are broken up and spread on the beds. In about a year the oysters have grown so much they have to be separated again. In about two more years they are mature enough to eat and the dredges bring them in.

Smoked Salmon Pate

Salmon pate highlights many of the finest restaurants in the world. This recipe will start off any meal well, but especially one you intend to be particularly elegant. Laced with watercress sauce, it looks as handsome as it tastes.

watercress
onion
smoked salmon
salmon fillets
dill
lemon juice
white pepper
salt
heavy cream
eggs
*watercress sauce ***

Butter a 3½ x 11½ x 2½ terrine* and line it with buttered parchment paper, buttered side up. Blanch **several sprigs watercress** for design and lay on a paper to dry; create your own design on the parchment paper in the terrine. Submerge 3½ oz watercress in boiling water for 15 seconds after which plunge it into cold water. Drain and squeeze dry; retain some juice for the recipe.

Preheat oven to 250°. In food processor mince **1 small onion.** Add **4 oz smoked salmon** (3 oz liquid smoke can be substituted), **6 3 oz salmon fillets** cut in 1" pieces, **2 t dill, 2 t lemon juice, ½ t white pepper, 1½ t salt;** mix till it forms a fine paste. With the machine running, slowly pour in **1¼ c heavy cream.** With machine still running add **2 large eggs** one at a time; process 30 seconds after eggs are added.

Next remove ¾ of mixture. To the remaining ¼ add blanched watercress by cutting through it until it is well blended. You now have some of the mixture with watercress and a larger amount without. Divide larger mixture in halves and put one half into terrine. Cut through it with a dull knife a few times and bang it twice to settle it.*

Place watercress mixture in a strip down center as evenly distributed as possible, and add remaining pate. Bang twice to settle. Cover pate with more buttered parchment paper and bake it in a water bath ¾ of the way up the pan for 15 minutes in 250° oven. After 15 minutes, turn heat down to 225° and bake for an additional 25 minutes. The pate will become firm — not hard.

When you remove it from the oven, wait for at least 5 minutes and then turn upside down on to a serving plate; then remove parchment paper.

When you serve it, lace each slice of pate diagonally with watercress sauce.

For watercress sauce see page 169.

A bread pan works nicely if you don't have a terrine.

To "bang" the pate, place your hands along the sides of the terrine, hit the bottom smartly on a table surface. This action aids in settling the pate.

Serves 12 to 16.

Stuffed Mushrooms

Make the stuffing for these mushrooms a day ahead of time; it tastes better after it sits for a day.

butter
olive oil
mushrooms
garlic
tabasco
sherry
salt
black pepper
parsley
paprika
basil
artichoke hearts
bread crumbs
parmesan
tomato wedges

Remove stems from **24 medium mushrooms** and chop stems fine. For stuffing melt **2 T butter** in **2 T olive oil** and saute chopped stems until they give up their juices.

Add **5 cloves garlic,** minced, **dash of tabasco;** simmer 1 minute. Add **¼ c sherry,** pouring it around edge of pan to deglaze.

Add **½ t salt, 1 t black pepper, 2 T chopped parsley, ¼ t paprika, 1 T basil, 4 to 5 chopped artichoke hearts.** Pour mixture over **2 c bread crumbs;** add **1¼ c grated parmesan,** and, if needed to shape mixture, more melted butter.

Fill caps so that stuffing mounds slightly. Brush outside with **olive oil.** Dip in **parmesan** for topping. Put **sherry** in bottom of baking dish, about ¼ **inch deep.**

Put mushrooms in baking dish. Bake at 375°.
When cheese topping melts and mushrooms
darken to gold, remove and serve with a
tomato wedge and a sprig of parsley.

Serves 6.

*Only two of
the Long Beach penin-
sula's turn-of-the-
century hotels still
stand. The Taylor Hotel
in Ocean Park, built in
1887, is on the list of
historic sites, but it no
longer rents rooms. The
Shelburne Hotel in Sea-
view, first built east of
the railroad tracks in
1896, was moved across
the road in 1911 and
attached to a board-
ing house that stood
there. Newly renovated
and furnished with an-
tiques, it still offers fif-
teen bedrooms and a
restaurant, which pro-
vided the first penin-
sular location for Nanci
and Jimella's tempting
food.*

Fried Cheese in Marinara Sauce

The sauce recipe is a standard one and a good one. Chef Lucas has served fried cheese with this sauce for many years – it has become a real favorite at many other restaurants throughout the Northwest. It is a striking and deliciously different appetizer and easy to prepare. Make the sauce ahead of time and fry the cheese just before you serve. Easy and different.

olive oil
onion
carrots
garlic
Italian plum tomatoes
oregano
basil
salt
pepper
butter
white wine
cheese of choice
eggs
milk
flour
cracker meal

Lightly brown in **¼ c olive oil 2 c onion,** coarsely chopped, **½ c carrots,** sliced, **4 cloves garlic,** minced, **4 c Italian plum tomatoes** (if fresh, 5 to 6 c). Sieve mixture and discard pulp; return to heat. Add **1 T oregano, 1 T fresh basil** (1 t dried), **salt,** freshly ground **pepper, 4 T butter, 1 c white wine.** Cook for 30 additional minutes.

Take **mozzarella, brie, camembert,** or **bel paese** — about **2 oz per person.**

Make egg dip with **2 to 3 eggs, 2 c milk;** stir. Cut cheese in wedges or strips. Dust lightly in flour; dip in egg wash then in fine cracker meal or bread crumbs.

Deep fry, quickly 1 minute, no more. Just to brown outside.

Lay cheese on individual dishes and lace sauce over.

Be careful not to cook cheese too long; all you'll be left with is a hollow shell.

Cover any remaining sauce and store for this or other dishes.

Oysters Italian

Some purists insist that oysters be eaten raw — no other way. They may be purists, but they don't ever get a chance to taste Oysters Italian.

oysters
brandy
garlic butter
parmesan
parsley
lemon wedges

Wash and shuck **24 oysters,** extra small grade. Clear both muscles, top and bottom, and return to shell.

Place oysters in the half-shell in a 1 x 9 x 13 baking pan. For seasoning you will need approximately ¼ **c brandy, ½ c garlic butter, ½ c parmesan cheese.**

Sprinkle each oyster with ½ **t brandy** and top with at least **1 t garlic butter** and **1 t parmesan.**

In preheated 425° oven, bake until cheese melts and oysters are gently poached in garlic butter, about 6 to 8 minutes.

Remove and place on serving dishes. Garnish with parsley and lemon wedges.

Serves 6.

Calamari Dijonnaise

The dijonnaise sauce coats the calamari dramatically and produces an incredible appetizer. If you're tired of run-of-the-mill appetizers, try Calamari Dijonnaise.

clarified butter
garlic
lemon
dijon mustard
white wine
heavy cream
calamari*
flour
parsley

Put **1½ oz clarified butter** in pan and, before it heats up, add **1 clove minced garlic.** Just before the garlic starts to burn, add **squeeze of lemon** to cool liquid. Blend carefully; add **1 T dijon mustard.** Deglaze pan with **¼ c white wine,** add no more than **3 T heavy cream,** blend and reduce enough to bring out color of mustard.

Heat oil in deep fryer to 360°.

Dust **calamari** with **flour.** Use approximately **2 oz of body rings** and **3 to 4 tentacles per serving.** (Multiply this amount by the number of guests you intend to serve.) Deep fry for 1 minute — no more than 1½ minutes.

When the calamari finish frying, coat with sauce and serve with **chopped parsley** and a **sprig of parsley** for a garnish.

You can use either fresh or frozen calamari, but if it is fresh, handle well because it is extremely perishable. First cut the tentacles and clean out the body debris. (Some people just cut the body and pound it as a fillet.) Keep the tentacles separate. For the bodies, hold the knife at a 45 degree angle and clear the viscera. Wash out the body cavity and cut it into smaller rings. Rinse well. To store them, squeeze a little lemon and drop the lemon right into the container.

Recipe is per serving: multiply as needed.

Scallops Nectarine

This dish is rather like a scallop margarita. The combination of the lime with the fruit and tequila plays off against the cream and cilantro with garlic and tabasco to produce a lovely combination. This recipe will serve one hearty appetizer appetite, two more judicious appetites.

clarified butter
scallops
flour
salt
pepper
tabasco
mushrooms
shallots
garlic
cilantro
lime juice
tequila
cream
nectarine
parmesan
triple sec
sour cream

In **4 T clarified butter,** saute **4 oz scallops,** lightly dusted in **flour.*** Salt, pepper to taste, with **dash of tabasco. Add ½ c mushrooms, 1 t chopped shallots, 1 t minced garlic, 1 t cilantro, 1 oz lime juice.** Marry.

Deglaze with **⅓ c tequila.** As it thickens, add **2 T cream, ½ nectarine,** cut into wedges. Sprinkle on **2 T parmesan,** freshly grated, and **1 to 2 T triple sec.**

Remove to platter and top with **dollop of sour cream,** generous **sprinkle of freshly chopped cilantro.**

The butter does not have to be searing hot; cook the scallops gently.

Recipe is per serving: multiply as needed.

Prawns with Pesto

5:30. The ARK kitchen starts to warm up. The white walls and stainless steel vie with the black iron stove tops for your eye. Dianne and Jennice stand by the eye level window waiting for their orders. Robin glides back and forth while Jimella stands at the stove. "I'm behind" warns Robin as he moves behind Carol who puts the finishing touches on salads. And Jimella flips a pan of Pesto Prawns to turn them. Your appetizer is nearly ready; here is Jimella's recipe for it.

prawns
butter
mushrooms
lemon
garlic
white wine
pesto*
tomatoes
onions
white pepper
salt
cream
parsley
tomatoes

Saute **4 oz prawns** in **clarified butter.** Add **½ c mushrooms,** squeeze **1 wedge lemon.** Brown lightly. Add **½ t garlic,** minced.* Deglaze with **⅓ c white wine.** Add **1½ T pesto.** Marry. Add **½ c diced tomatoes, 2 green onions,** sliced thin, **white pepper, salt, to taste.** Add **1 T cream** at end. Garnish with **chopped parsley, chopped tomatoes.**

See page 170 for pesto recipe.

Keep pan moving to keep from burning.

Recipe is per serving: multiply as needed.

Mediterranean Oyster Loaf

Back when the oysters from Willapa were plentiful and inexpensive, the dish was called poor man's pizza; now oysters are somewhat less plentiful, somewhat more expensive — and are certainly considered a delicacy. Oyster loaf becomes a high class preparation, indeed. So easy to prepare, so wonderful to serve and eat.

french bread
tomato
green onions
black olives
stuffed green olives
garlic
parsley
thyme
capers
salt
pepper
lemon
tabasco
olive oil
oysters
fish stock
sherry
parmesan

Cut in half and scoop out inside of both halves of a **1 lb loaf french bread** — hollow halves out, much like bread canoes. Grind bread from insides to medium fine crumbs. Combine with **1 tomato,** finely diced, **4 green onions,** finely sliced, **½ c each black and stuffed green olives, 6 cloves garlic,** minced, **2 T chopped parsley, pinch thyme, 2 T capers, salt, pepper to taste, juice of 1 lemon, 3 dashes tabasco, 2 T olive oil.** Mix well, tossing.

Poach **2 c extra small oysters** in **fish stock** or in **water** with **sherry.** Place oysters in liquid; bring to boil. Cook 3 to 4 minutes. Drain immediately. Chop coarsely; add to bread mixture. Mix well. Add **½ c parmesan;** toss.

Brush **olive oil lightly** on hollowed out space of bread, particularly the edges. Pack mixture into hollow of bread (it should be firm, a bit mounded in center, even with bread on sides of loaf.) Place halves with oyster mix back together as though bread were whole.*

Wrap tightly with foil. Refrigerate overnight or for 24 hours. Cut ¼ to ½ inch slices with serrated knife to serve. Garnish with **black olives** and **parsley.**

To reassemble loaves, place them side by side and roll up to each other. Do not attempt to place one on top of the other.

Variation: use shrimp instead of oysters, or use no seafood at all.

Serves 12 to 24.

he descendants of the pioneers of Oysterville still remember its glory. A son of one of the founders — Cecil Espy who died in 1982 at the age of 94 — said visitors used to be greeted with the verse:

Said one oyster to another
In tones of pure delight,
"I will meet you in the kitchen
And we'll both get stewed tonight."

Ceviche

Do you have a youngster with you this afternoon? As Valerie seated you, she no doubt gave the child a coloring book — children's menu. By the time your young friend had a chance to look through it, Valerie had brought a water glass with color crayons. What Valerie likely didn't tell you is that, not only does she serve as hostess some meals and waitress for others, but also she does graphic art work — the coloring book, for example.

Valerie isn't the only serving person who makes more than one contribution to the restaurant. Kaaren, a delegate to the national AAUW Convention, is in charge of the wine cellar; she is an expert on Oregon and Washington state wines. Laurie has done considerable painting and maintenance.

Jennice not only serves at table and acts as hostess; she also tends bar. (Her husband, by the way, made all the window boxes.) Diane makes posters and also did the menu design; in addition, she teaches folk dancing and graphic art in her spare time.

Cat works at THE ARK only in the summer; she attends the University of Hawaii for the rest of the year. During the summer, though, she catches up. She serves as a hostess and waits table during the day.

If you should arrive at THE ARK at about 5 a.m., you'll not find an empty restaurant. No indeed. Those spotless floors and carpets don't just happen. John, who also came with the restaurant when Nanci and Jimella arrived, comes in the wee hours when it's still dark to make THE ARK sparkling clean and comfortable for you.

Perhaps you never thought about it, but it takes a family like THE ARK family to make a meal like an ARK meal.

snapper or
scallops

yellow onion

jalapeno
pepper

oregano

salt

black pepper

cilantro

limes

lemons

olive oil

bell peppers

tomatoes

Cut **1½ lbs snapper and/or scallops** into thin bite-sized pieces. Marinate a minimum of 2 hours in a plastic or glass container (not metal) in the following marinade: **½ small yellow onion,** ground fine, **1½ small jalapeno pepper without seeds,** chopped fine, **½ t oregano, ½ t salt, black pepper,** fresh ground, **1 T cilantro,** finely chopped, **juice of 4 to 6 limes, juice of 1 to 2 lemons, ¼ c olive oil.**

Before serving add diced **bell pepper** and **tomato.**

For salad, place on a bed of chopped lettuce with bell peppers and tomatoes mixed with wedges of avocado as garnish.

Chef Lucas, for special occasions, serves the ceviche on a ½ avocado as a cup. Use a wedge of tomato as garnish.

Serves 6 to 8.

The most interesting customs shared by many Indian tribes of the Pacific Northwest was the potlach. The word drives from the Chinook word "pat-shatl," which means to give away. The potlach was a social affair at which one tribe or group demonstrated its status, wealth and power by giving away large quantities of prized goods (blankets, animal skins, copper artifacts) to rival tribes. Often goods were simply destroyed. To preserve their own honor and status, the guests at a potlach were obligated to reciprocate in the future.

The potlach was often very competitive and the hosts attempted to humiliate their rivals by offering more food than could be consumed. In great eating contests large bowls of food (sometimes even canoes full of food!) were presented to the guests. The visitors had to eat it all to preserve their honor; the hosts had to have more food on hand than the guests could possibly eat.

NOTES

Soups & Salads

WILLIE KEIL — UNIQUE PIONEER

More than a century ago pioneers arrived
in the Willapa Bay area in various ways: north
from California, west down the Columbia,
overland from the midwest. But Willie Keil
was the only one to start and arrive literally
and genuinely pickled. In 1855 Willie's father
organized a group of Christian communists
who planned a settlement on the southeastern
shores of the Bay, and William Keil, Sr. pro-
mised his 21-year-old son that he could lead
the 34-wagon caravan across the Oregon Trail.
Unfortunately, a week before the group was to
start, Willie died. Not a man to break a promise, the senior Keil laid Willie in a coffin,
covered him with whiskey, placed him at the
head of the caravan, and headed west.
Although 1855 was a bad year for covered
wagons and at several places the settlers were
advised to turn back because of the massacres
that had occurred, they kept on, safeguarded
by hymns, prayers, and Willie. The Indians
they met were respectful and friendly. When
they arrived at Willapa six months later, they
buried Willie, whose grave is still mentioned,
without comment, on some Washington road
maps. What happened to the whiskey on
those long, cold, rainy nights — weather that
persuaded the commune to move on to the
Willamette Valley, finally leaving Willie
behind — is not recorded.

Onion Soup

This recipe cuts some of the time out of the traditional French Onion soup preparation, but makes "one wonderful French Onion soup." Serve it with a bottle of hearty red wine and a salad on a rainy, stormy beach day.

onions
butter
beef base
dry vermouth
beef consomme
beef stock
celery
bay leaves
croutons
gruyere

Cut ends off **5 onions,** peel, cut in half across the grain. Slice onion into ⅛" to ¼" slices. (Cutting onion this way will allow it to withstand high temperature and still retain its shape.)

Put **8 to 10 oz cold butter** into saute pan and place onions on top. Saute onions on medium heat until butter and onion have produced nectar — about 20 minutes. When onions are golden brown (or carmelized), stir in **3 oz of high quality beef base.**

Add ⅔ **c dry vermouth*** at medium high temperature. Add **3 c beef consomme.** Add **3 qts beef stock, 1 cracked celery rib,* 3 bay leaves.**

Turn temperature to high, bring to boil, lower temperature to maintain a low simmering rumble for about 20 minutes to reduce soup.

To serve, set rack high in oven and set temperature at 450°. Ladle out a nice distribution of soup and onions into oven-proof bowls. Spread one layer of **plain croutons** or **day-old bread** cut in small cubes. On top of this, sprinkle about **½ c shredded gruyere** per serving. Heat until the cheese browns — 8 to 10 minutes.

As you work the vermouth in, the aromatic hit tells you what you've got. Stop and appreciate it.

To crack celery, don't break it all the way through; the flavor will seep out during the entire cooking process.

You may find that you have more soup than you need for a particular meal; that's okay, the soup matures well. If you wish to freeze your extra soup, place it in an air-tight plastic container. The oil that rises from the soup as it cools will seal the soup nicely. Remember: allow the soup to cool first in the refrigerator before placing it in the freezer.

Bouillabaisse

This recipe makes a lot of soup. Prepare for a big party; you won't regret the leftovers. You will never taste a better bouillabaisse. Chef Jimella Lucas says "I have never given out this recipe, but felt that I wanted it in my very own cookbook."

onions
celery
bell peppers
butter
cumin
oregano
sweet basil
garlic
fennel
celery seed
coriander
bay leaves
sage
cayenne
fish bouillon*
tomatoes
tomato puree
sauterne
fish stock*
seafood of choice*
aioli sauce*

Peel and cut off the ends of **5 onions.** Cut bottom off **½ bunch celery** (6 to 7 good sized ribs). Clean seeds and membrane from **3 bell peppers.** Run vegetables through food grinder to chop fine. (Don't puree them.)

Saute vegetables with **8 oz butter** — in the stock pot you'll be using — about 10 to 15 minutes. Be sure to stir vegetables occasionally to keep them from sticking to bottom of pan.*

Measure into bowl **3 T cumin, ¼ c oregano, ¼ c sweet basil, 5 T minced garlic, 5 T whole fennel, 3 T celery seed, 2 T whole coriander, 3 bay leaves, 3 T sage, ½ t cayenne.** Add spices to vegetables. Add **1 c fish bouillon** and blend it in well.*

Add **4 c diced tomatoes** (Canned; if fresh, take tomatoes through a water bath and peel.), **4 c tomato puree** and blend till you have a paste.

Put in **1 qt sauterne** and allow it to marry with mixture.

Add **2 gal fish stock** and bring to rumbling boil over high temperature.

Reduce temperature and simmer with low rumbling boil for 30 minutes. (You may want to give the soup another 10 to 15 minutes to reduce.)

Cut the **fish you choose** into chunks (larger chunks for whitefish so it doesn't disintegrate.)

Just before you're ready to serve, add fish and cook for 2 to 3 minutes.

Serve with a generous **dollop of aioli sauce** in each bowl.

This is bouillabaisse.

For fish stock recipe, see page 182; for aioli sauce, page 176.

In this recipe you may choose the quantity and type of seafood to use: e.g., crab legs, clams, mussels, prawns, scallops, whitefish, sturgeon, salmon, halibut. Chef Lucas suggests the following quantities of seafood per serving: 2 sections of crab body, 1 or 2 crab legs, 2 prawns, 4 to 5 oz scallops, 1 or 2 chunks salmon or whitefish.

You'll need a big stock pot for this recipe.

You can use pieces of chicken breast in addition to the seafood.

You can find good quality fish bouillon in specialty food stores.

Seafood Chowder

THE ARK serves a traditional Boston Clam Chowder dubbed by many to be one of the best on the West coast. Chef Lucas says modestly that "you won't get raves from any true Bostonians on this aberrant form of chowder, but you will have a wonderful winter soup. Its ingredients can be interesting, filling, and rich flavored; if you keep fish stock on hand, it is quite easily assembled."

butter
celery
onions
carrots
green peppers
garlic
dry sherry
salt
pepper
marjoram
thyme
tomatoes
fish stock*
roux*
potatoes
snapper
chowder
clams

In soup pot, over medium high heat, melt **½ c butter.** Add diced vegetables, **3 c onions, 1½ c carrots, ½ medium sized green pepper, 1 c celery, 6 cloves minced garlic.** Saute until vegetables are tender, about 10 minutes, stirring occasionally. Add **½ c dry sherry, salt and pepper, 1 T marjoram, 1 T whole thyme,** and **3 c fresh diced tomatoes** with juice from dicing included. Let marry well for 3 to 5 minutes.

Add **6 c fish stock** and bring to a gentle boil.

Add **3 T roux;** simmer 5 to 10 minutes, or until mixture thickens.

If it doesn't thicken to your taste, you may add more roux, a T at a time, cooking for a few minutes before adding more. Cook soup about 10 minutes over medium heat, stirring frequently to keep vegetables off bottom.

Add **1½ c raw potatoes,** peeled and diced, and cook over medium heat until they are turning tender. Raise the heat to a rumbling boil and add **½ to ¾ lbs snapper fillets,** cut into 1 inch pieces. Cook at rolling boil four minutes, add **chowder clams,** cook for a minute and serve.

Sprinkle lightly with chopped parsley; serve with crackers or french bread.

For roux recipe, see page 26.

Chef Lucas notes, "Because this soup is basically considered a broth, you can hold the soup by delaying the addition of fish, simply lower heat and keep warm. The types of fish available for the recipe are limitless. This type of chowder is often referred to as 'poorman's bouillabaisse' because you can, (as the last addition), add little neck clams in shell, mussels, cooked crawfish, prawns, one inch pieces of salmon, dungeness crab, etc. As you can see, it is truly a soup regulated by the 'catch of the day.' "

For fish stock recipe, see page 182.

Serves 10 to 12.

Oyster Stew

This one is a classic; at THE ARK, the diner eats the stew while looking out at the bay that the oysters came from. The recipe is per serving.

shallots

clarified butter

salt

black pepper

tabasco

oysters

sherry

half and half

butter

parsley

Lightly cook in skillet **1 t minced shallots** in **1 oz clarified butter, salt and pepper to taste, 1 dash tabasco.** When shallots are tender, add **6 extra-small oysters** which have been washed in cold water. Blend into other ingredients and heat. Keep pan moving so as not to make oysters tough on edges. When oysters start firming on edges, deglaze with **lace of sherry (not more than 1 t)** and add **1½ to 2 c half and half** immediately. Leave heat on high, moving pan so heat distributes.*

With slotted spoon, remove oysters to bowl and pour cream over. Top with a **dollop of butter** and a **sprinkling of chopped parsley.**

You want cream to be intensely hot but *never* to boil.

Recipe is per serving: multiply as needed.

"*H*e was a bold man that first [ate] an oyster," wrote Jonathan Swift in the eighteenth century. Whoever he was, those who feast at The Ark owe him a belated debt of gratitude.

Cranberry Chicken Salad

Put 28 cranberry farms on the peninsula together with Chef Lucas' imagination and you come up with striking new combinations like this adaption of the American classic.

chicken
celery
apples
walnuts
capers
mayonnaise
dijon mustard
celery seeds
cranberries
fresh ginger
orange
lemon
cranberry
sauce

Toss together **3 c cooked chicken** cut up, **¾ c chopped celery, 1½ c chopped apples, ¾ c chopped walnuts, 1 to 2 T capers.** Mix with **1 c homemade mayonnaise** to which you have added **2 T dijon mustard, ½ t whole celery seeds.**

Grind **1 c whole cranberries, ¾ t fresh ginger, 1 small orange,** peel and all, with **½ lemon.**

Mix with **¼ c whole cranberry sauce.**

Combine cranberry and chicken mixtures.

Let set for at least an hour before serving.

Serves 6 to 8.

Zucchini Cod Salad

If you leave out the cod, you have Zucchini Salad.

vinaigrette *
zucchini
carrots
daikon
radishes
red onion
red pepper
red radishes
cod fillets
green onions
leaf lettuce
black olives
lemon wedges
parsley

Begin by preparing **vinaigrette sauce** if you don't have any on hand.

Julienne **1½ c zucchini, 1 c carrots, 1 c daikon radishes;** blanch in boiling water for 1 to 1½ minutes till tender, not soft. Put in ice water bath. Finely dice **½ red onion,** julienne **½ small red pepper,** slice **½ c red radishes.**

Combine blanched vegetables with red onion, red pepper, red radishes. Toss together with about ½ **c vinaigrette;** marinate.

Heat water in steam pot (a steamer in a saucepan is fine); when liquid boils, reduce heat so liquid simmers intensely. Place several diagonally cut **2 oz cod fillets** * in steamer. Put lid on; steam for 2 to 3 (not more than 4) minutes. Remove cod immediately with slotted spoon; place in refrigerator to cool.

When cod chills, assemble salad. First, toss **3 green onions,** thinly sliced, into vegetable mixture, place **leaf lettuce** on a chilled plate as background, place vegetables on lettuce, place cod on top. Dribble a bit more **vinaigrette** on cod, garnish with **black olives, lemon wedges,** and streaks of **parsley** on fish.

See page 180 for vinaigrette.

The parts of the salad are easily prepared well in advance of the serving time.

To steam cod, use water with a squeeze of lemon, water alone, or water with a little bit of fish stock.

Serves 6 to 8.

he main treasures the casual beachcomber finds among the driftwood are bits of pumice washed down the river from the 1981 eruption of Mt. St. Helens; or, for those with a fancy for shells, there are lovely bleached white sand dollars at Lead-better Point, each with a five-petalled flower on top and five filigree bones that look like tiny birds hidden inside.

Mediterranean Salad

You need 4 to 24 hours for marination, but what a treat for a salad lover.

olive oil
red wine vinegar
lemon
salt
black pepper
garlic
dijon mustard
sugar
oranges
red onion
leaf lettuce
black olives

Prepare vinaigrette by combining **½ c olive oil, ¼ c red wine vinegar, juice of 1 lemon, salt and pepper to taste, 2 cloves of garlic,** crushed, **¼ t dijon mustard, 1 T sugar, 3 small cloves garlic,** bled.*

Peel **2 medium sized oranges,** slice horizontally (across the wedges) into ¼" thick slices.

Slice **½ red onion** into thin rounds.

Pour vinaigrette over orange and onion slices. Cover and store over night (at least 4 hours, 24 hours if possible).

When you are ready to serve, place orange and onion slices on a bed of 3 to 4 arranged **lettuce leaves,** garnished with **black olives,** sliced into rings. Just before serving, strain liquid, and serve in small pitcher.

To bleed garlic, peel it and cut it to the core in 2 or 3 places just before adding to the vinaigrette.

Serves 4.

Sauteed Zucchini Milam

This recipe is from the accomplished qualities of ARK apprentice Robin Milam, who has developed a delightfully delicate touch.

clarified butter	Heat **3 T clarified butter** in medium saute
zucchini	skillet. Add **3 c zucchini,** sliced, **salt, pep-**
salt	**per to taste, juice of ½ lemon, 3 cloves**
white pepper	**garlic,** minced, **1 t shallots, ¼ t whole thyme.** Let ingredients marry into heat; add
lemon	¼ **c white wine** just when butter starts to
garlic	brown. Right before zucchini becomes tender,
shallots	add **½ c diced tomatoes.** Cook 30 seconds
thyme	and serve immediately. Total cooking time, 5
white wine	minutes.
tomatoes	Serves 6 to 8.

***B**eard's Hollow, on the ocean side of the peninsula, is named for Captain E. N. Beard, master of the Vandalia, whose dead body washed ashore in that cove in 1853.*

Acini

Acini is a small, barley-sized pasta usually used in soups. Prepared like this, it is wonderful with Chicken Mediterranean and with fish dishes also.

acini
clarified butter
salt
white pepper
mushrooms
green onions
garlic
parsley

Heat **3 T clarified butter** in skillet and add **2 c cooked acini.*** Season with **salt and white pepper to taste.** Add **½ c chopped mushrooms, ¼ c thinly sliced green onions, 2 cloves garlic,** minced, **¼ t chopped parsley.**

Move pan constantly to prevent contents from sticking. Cook until the vegetables are cooked through, but not mushy.

Be sure the ingredients are chopped and measured ahead of time.

Have the acini itself prepared before starting your main dish. Cook until al dente (about 4 to 6 minutes) in boiling water, rinse in cold water immediately, drain and hold until you are ready to use it. Then just before the meal is ready to serve, assemble this acini dish.

Serves 4.

NOTES

Entrees

SPLIT THE SALMON
DOWN THE BACK . . .

According to Chinook legend, while old man South Wind was travelling north a long, long time ago, he met an ogress. When he asked her for food, she gave him a net and told him to catch his own fish. He caught a little whale. But just as he was about to cut it with his knife, the ogress cried out, "Don't cut it crossways. Take a sharp shell and split it down the back." He paid no attention, and as soon as he cut the fish across the side it turned into an enormous bird, so huge that its flying obscured the sun and the noise of its wings shook the earth. The thunderbird flew to the top of Saddleback Mountain and laid its eggs. When the ogress found Thunderbird's nest, she broke the eggs and threw them down the mountain. Every egg became a Chinook Indian. That's how the tribe began, and that's why the first salmon caught every year must be split down the back. If the salmon is cut the wrong way, the run will cease and no more will be caught that year.

The legend goes on to say that Thunderbird and South Wind looked for the ogress and never found her. Still, they travel north together every year.

Salmon Lucas

This dish proudly bears the name of the chef, Jimella Lucas. She is quite fussy about using only peaches at their peak. If you find yours not perfect, you might add 1 T peach flavored brandy to the sauce as it cooks. The cranberry puree needs to be ready before hand, so plan well; have some available all the time, for once you eat this entree, you'll want to fix Salmon Lucas often.

The recipe is for each serving; for additional servings, simply multiply the ingredients accordingly.

clarified butter
fresh salmon
flour
lemon
salt
white pepper
mushrooms
garlic
brandy
heavy cream
dijon mustard
peaches
cranberry puree*
parsley

Heat **3 T clarified butter** in skillet*. Dust lightly with **flour 6 oz fresh salmon,** cut into ¼ inch fillets; brown slightly on one side in heated butter. Add **juice from lemon wedge; salt, white pepper to taste.** As you turn salmon, add **¼c sliced fresh mushrooms, pinch of fresh garlic,** minced. Brown second side gently.

Deglaze pan with **3 T brandy.** Add ½ c **heavy cream, 1 t dijon mustard, ½ fresh peach,** peeled and sliced. Marry mustard and cream by moving pan in circular motion.

Remove to serving dish and pour sauce over, arranging peaches on top. Top each serving with **2 t cranberry puree;** sprinkle lightly with chopped parsley.

Cranberry puree: Put 1 c fresh or frozen cranberries, 1 t granulated sugar, and squeeze of lemon juice in container or blender or food processor; puree well. You can use this puree or Cranberry Grand Marnier Sauce on page 166.

Do not have butter so hot as to crisp salmon when you put it in.

Move pan steadily to keep the food from sticking.

Chef Lucas serves this dish with white rice.

Recipe is per serving: multiply as needed.

n 1805 William Clark noted in his journal that he killed a salmon and "saw in my ramble to day a red berry," that some authorities identify as the wild cranberry. It is a shame he never thought to combine the two taste treats. The results are very special, as anyone who has tasted Salmon Lucas can testify.

Stuffed Salmon Florentine

Many people think that with the salmon nature achieved its zenith; Stuffed Salmon Florentine displays this elegant food without detracting from its light and delicate flavor. When you are going to serve it, be sure to allow time to prepare and refrigerate the filling. Also, remember to prepare the bread crumbs ahead of time.

unsalted butter
flour
milk
salt
white pepper
sherry
fresh spinach

Heat **1½ T unsalted butter** in saucepan; sprinkle **2 T flour** over it. Cook flour-butter mixture until it loses its starchy flavor — 3 to 5 minutes. Add **¾ c milk,** room temperature, seasoned with **salt, white pepper to taste.** Cook over moderate heat, stirring constantly. Once sauce grows thick and smooth (about a minute) add **2 T sherry,** stir and set aside.

unsalted butter
scallions
yellow onions
mushrooms
sweet basil
dried oregano
whole dried thyme
parmesan
salmon fillets
lemon
*seasoned bread crumbs**

Drain well **10 oz fresh spinach,** chopped and blanched* and put in clean saucepan with **6 T unsalted butter.** Chop **3 scallions, ½ c yellow onions, 1 c mushrooms;** blend together and add to saucepan. Add **1 t dried sweet basil, 1 t dried oregano, ¼ t whole dried thyme;** mix well.

Saute over medium heat, stirring frequently. After 5 minutes, add **½ c parmesan,** freshly grated. Stir over heat for about 5 minutes until cheese melts and blends in. Combine with white sauce, taste for seasoning and cover. Refrigerate until it jells—between 2 and 4 hours.

clarified butter
white wine
lemon slices
parsley

Cut a slit in the side of each of **6 6 oz salmon fillets** to make a pocket; leave ¼ inch intact at each end. Squeeze **lemon juice** over each.

Open each slit gently; place filling into cavity carefully*. Place stuffed salmon in large, shallow baking dish. Distribute evenly over the fillets ½ **c seasoned bread crumbs.** Drizzle with ½ **c clarified butter.** Cover bottom of pan with ½ **c white wine;** bake in 425⁰ oven for 10 to 15 minutes*, until salmon is flaky. Serve with garnish of **lemon slices** and **parsley.**

For seasoned bread crumbs, see page 26.

To blanch spinach, place it in a colander. Put the colander in a bowl or pot large enough to hold the colander, pour boiling water ove and let it stand in the water for 1½ minutes. Take it out and hold it till it's needed.

Use toothpicks to secure slits in fillets if necessary.

Be careful: do not overcook salmon; time will depend on the thickness of the fillets.

Serves 6.

Sturgeon Dijonnaise

Fresh sturgeon are taken virtually from the back door of THE ARK, the largest supply coming from the mouth of the Columbia. Between the beginning of July and the end of September this last of the prehistoric fish comes right from the bay. It's an ugly fish: it looks like a giant sucker, growing up to 7 feet long. But don't judge a book by its cover, the cliche goes: this fish produces the very most authentic cavier from Russia and the flesh has a firm unusual texture, almost like land animal meat, with a flavor that defies description. You need only 4 oz per serving of this fish because it is so rich; serve each person 2 2 oz fillets.

sturgeon fillets	Lightly dust with **flour 4 2 oz fillets of**
flour	**sturgeon.*** Heat **4 to 6 T clarified butter**
clarified butter	in skillet. Place fillets in hot butter, add ¾ **c**
mushrooms	**sliced mushrooms, ¼ c sliced onions,**
onions	**salt, white pepper to taste,** a **squeeze of**
salt	**lemon wedge, 1 dash tabasco.**
white pepper	Let fish cook on one side at high heat for 2 to
lemon	3 minutes. Turn over; add **½ t garlic,** minc-
tabasco	ed, **2 t capers, 1 t dijon mustard, ⅓ c**
garlic	**white wine.**
capers	Agitate pan to marry mustard with rest of
dijon mustard	sauce, cooking fish 2 to 3 minutes more.
white wine	While it cooks, add **¼ c sherry, ¼ c heavy**
sherry	**cream,** marry with rest of sauce. Add **⅓ c**
heavy cream	**fresh diced tomatoes, 3 green onions,**
tomatoes	sliced thin.
green onions	THE ARK serves this wonderful dish with rice pilaf.

It's important to have all the ingredients ready before you start cooking. It goes quickly once you get started.

Don't do any more than 2 servings per skillet.

Be sure the excess flour is off because it will burn.

Test fish for doneness with your hand; it will get firm around the outside part first. The more firm the fish is, the more done it is. It will get the consistency almost of meat.

If the sauce is still thin when the fish is ready, simply remove fish to the serving plate. Keep it warm and continue to reduce sauce. You want the sauce to be thick enough to cover the fish and a little bit more; you don't want a soupy plate.

Serves 2.

Sturgeon with Garlic Raspberry Sauce

At the nationally acclaimed Garlic Festival in 1983, the entree described as "a breathtaking success" by one reviewer was the Sturgeon with Raspberry Sauce. It stands as a monument to the imagination of Chef Lucas whose genius at bringing together unlikely fish and fruit combinations has elicited high praise from James Beard and others.

clarified butter

sturgeon

flour

salt

pepper

lemon

garlic

shallots

raspberry wine vinegar

madeira

raspberry sauce*

cream

raspberries

In **2 to 3 T clarified butter,** saute **6 oz sturgeon fillet,** dusted lightly in **flour. Salt, pepper to taste.** Add **squeeze of lemon.** Remove fillet to pan and put in oven, 425⁰. Add **½ t garlic,** minced, **½ t shallots,** minced, **1 T raspberry wine vinegar.** Deglaze with **3 T madeira.**

Add **3 T raspberry sauce, 1 T cream.** Allow to mix well. Lace over sturgeon. Garnish with **3 to 4 fresh raspberries.**

Serve with white rice.

Raspberry Sauce:

Cook **10 oz raspberries** in **2 T to ¼ c water** and a squeeze of lemon till slightly thickened. Sieve out seeds.

Recipe is per serving: multiply as needed.

Snapper with Capers

This is an unusual way of serving snapper; the Italian flavor complements the fish flavor surprisingly well: it's a much more delicate serving than you might predict.

eggs
half and half
or whole milk
snapper fillets
flour
clarified butter
white wine
garlic
parsley
lemon
fish stock
capers
seasoned bread
crumbs *
parsley
lemon wedges

Beat **3 eggs** lightly with **½ c half and half or whole milk.** Place **4 6 oz snapper fillets** (sea bass would also work well) in egg mixture and let them rest until they absorb some liquid.

Dust fillets with **flour;** be sure to remove excess as it will burn. Saute fillets for 3 minutes on each side in **4 to 5 oz clarified butter.*** Remove fillets to warm platter. Deglaze pan with **½ c white wine;** add **¼ t minced garlic, ¼ t fresh chopped parsley, juice of ½ lemon, 3 oz fish stock.** Reduce about a third; it will have a syrupy texture.

Add **2 T capers.** Lace sauce over fillets; sprinkle oven browned **seasoned bread crumbs** over fish. Serve with **lemon wedges, fresh chopped parsley** as garnish.

The recipe for seasoned bread crumbs is on page 26.

If the butter should get to hot, wash it with white wine to reduce the temperature.

Serves 4.

Steamed Ling Cod with Dill Sauce

A winter storm on Willapa Bay; the spray bouncing against the picturesque boats outside the windows; waves splashing across the thin roadway to the oyster building—all these and steamed ling cod with hot dill sauce at THE ARK make a memorable experience. If you have to miss the storm, at least you can have the cod.

milk
dill weed
dijon mustard
sherry
roux*
cod
lemon

Heat **2 c milk** in a saucepan; do not boil. Add **1 T dill weed** (or 2 T fresh chopped dill), **1½ t dijon mustard, ¼ c sherry, 3 to 4 T roux.** Cook till incorporated. When sauce is ready, float a pad of butter on top to keep it from forming a crust.

Steam **1 5 oz piece of ling cod per person.*** You can also use perch, sable fish, cod, or even salmon. Steam cod for 5 to 6 minutes over water with a **squeeze of lemon** added.

Lace sauce over fish and serve immediately.

For roux recipe, see page 26.

Steaming removes the oil in the fish, making for a really delicate fish dish. You could use a combination of fish stock and water to steam the fish, but be careful not to make the stock mix too rich because it will overwhelm the delicacy of the ling cod.

Recipe is per serving: multiply as needed.

Sole with Pesto

James Beard has published this recipe in 102 different newspapers in the United States and Canada; it is a striking combination with a buttery, delicate fish and bold sauce.

eggs
half and half
or whole milk
petrale sole*
flour
clarified butter
white wine
pesto sauce*

Beat **3 eggs** lightly with **½ c half and half or whole milk.** Place **4 5 to 6 oz fillets of petrale sole** in egg mixture and let them rest until they have absorbed some liquid.

Dust fillets with **flour.*** Saute quickly in **2 oz clarified butter** — about 2 minutes on one side and one minute on the other — and remove to a warm platter.

Keep fillets warm while deglazing pan with **¼ c dry white wine,** loosening residue. Simmer while adding **3 T pesto sauce** and another touch of wine. Blend sauce quickly.

Pour sauce over fish; serve immediately.

For pesto sauce see recipe on page 170.

You may substitute flounder, lemon sole, or snapper for petrale sole.

When dusting fillets, remove extra flour as any excess will burn.

Serves 4.

Sauteed Halibut with Artichoke Hearts

This dish is not only good to look at, but it also has that special ARK effect on the palate.

clarified butter

flour

fillets of halibut

salt

white pepper

dry sherry

shallots

garlic

lemon

mushrooms

dijon mustard

heavy cream

artichoke hearts

hollandaise sauce*

parsley

Heat **¾ c clarified butter; flour 4   6 oz fillets of halibut.** When butter becomes medium hot, brown them 3 to 4 minutes on first side. Add **salt, white pepper to taste.** Repeat on second side, for slightly less time. Remove fillets to baking dish; place them in 425⁰ oven for 4 minutes.

Complete sauce by deglazing pan with **½ c dry sherry;*** add to pan residue **3 shallots,** chopped fine, **2 cloves garlic,** minced, **juice of ½ lemon, 1 c sliced mushrooms, 2 T dijon mustard, ½ c heavy cream,* 4 whole artichoke hearts.**

Reduce sauce till creamy.*

Lace sauce over fillets. Serve with dollop of **hollandaise** and **chopped parsley** on top.

—

For hollandaise sauce recipe, see page 173.

Be ready with an additional ¼ c dry sherry in case you need a little more in the sauce.

When you make the sauce, you might find that you want a little more cream; if so, add ¼ c half and half.

If fillets come ready before the sauce reduces sufficiently, simply keep them warm.

If you want a special touch, cut the artichoke hearts in half and place two halves on each fillet, cut side down.

Serves 4.

From the earliest days wrecks have been a boon to the inhabitants of the peninsula. The Indians collected camphorwood chests and copper washed ashore from Oriental junks; white settlers got silverware, flour, gold pieces, liquor, lumber, Stetson hats, lard, even pianos. According to one writer, pioneer children went to bed praying, "God bless Pa and Ma and bring a wreck in on our beach."

Want a stunning gourmet delight, but don't have time right now? It you have tartar sauce on hand and halibut fillets, this recipe's your answer. Serve with steamed vegetable and/or a simple green salad. Wonderful.

halibut fillets *lemon*	Place **4 6 oz fillets of halibut,** center cut, in baking pan.
tartar sauce* *celery* *paprika* *white wine*	Squeeze **juice of ½ lemon** over fillets and cover with **2 to 3 oz tartar sauce per fillet.** Top with **½ c finely chopped celery, sprinkling of paprika.**
	Place **½ c white wine** in pan, bake on bottom rack of oven at 425⁰ for 12 to 15 minutes.

For tartar sauce recipe, see page 171.

Serves 4.

Clam Fritters

This is a recipe that pays proper respect to the razor clams dug on the beaches near THE ARK. Obtaining a razor clam requires much stomping and ceremony. Serve them with Vermont maple syrup; they are wonderful anytime — but extra fine for a special breakfast.

butter
onions
eggs
flour
cream
bread crumbs
clams
celery
parsley
salt
thyme
garlic
paprika
tabasco
white pepper
dry mustard
lemon butter*
maple syrup

Melt **4 T butter** in skillet. Stir and simmer **½ c minced onions** until golden but not brown. Remove from heat.

Combine **5 eggs** with ¾ **c flour.** Slowly stir in **1 c cream** and then **1 c soft bread crumbs.** Add sauteed onions.

Add **3 c finely chopped clams, 1 c finely minced celery, ¼ c finely chopped parsley.**

Stir in **1 t salt, ½ t thyme, 1 t fresh chopped garlic, 1 t paprika, dash tabasco, ¼ t white pepper, ½ t dry mustard.**

Let batter rest 1 hour. Drop by ladling onto greased grill. Serve with whipped lemon butter and warm maple syrup.

Make lemon butter by grating 1 t lemon rind into 1 c softened butter and beating until pale yellow and airy.

Pipe the whipped butter in a swirl design across the fritters and sprinkle chopped parsley over for a special presentation.

Chef Main says: "I have found that hand chopped veggies look and taste better in this recipe vs. food processor ones. The cut is cleaner and defines the taste better."

Variation: achieve a more delicate flavor by substituting dill for thyme. Garnish with fresh dill across butter.

Shrimp Avocado Quiche

Note that the pate brisee crust needs to be ready ahead of time for this unusual and elegant dish. In fact, the pate brisee, the batter and filling can be made a day ahead of time and refrigerated till you're ready. Be sure to allow enough time after baking, too; it needs to rest for a full 15 minutes so it will cut perfectly at the table. From making the pate brisee to cutting and serving the quiche, this is a class act; fun to prepare, beautiful to serve and a joy to eat.

eggs
egg yolks
dijon mustard
salt
white pepper
tabasco
nutmeg
heavy cream

Batter

Combine **6 eggs, 3 egg yolks** in a large bowl and whisk until blended. Mix in **1 T dijon mustard, ½ t salt, ¼ t white pepper, 3 shakes tabasco, ¼ t fresh nutmeg,** grated. Add **1½ c heavy cream;** whisk gently until incorporated.

butter
mushrooms
garlic
sherry
green onions
shrimp
avocado
gruyere
parmesan

pate brisee*

Filling

Melt **2 T butter** in sauce pan. When it begins to bubble, add **¼ c sliced mushrooms, 2 cloves garlic,** minced. As soon as mushrooms begin to give up their juices, pour **⅛ to ¼ c sherry** around edge of pan, continue to simmer for one minute. Remove from heat and add **¼ c chopped green onions.**

Cool. Once cooled, add **4 oz shrimp,** cleaned and cooked. Divide **1 avocado** in half and cut each half lengthwise into 4 equal slices. Skin slices.

Put on frozen quiche crust, **1½ c (4 to 5 oz) gruyere,** grated coarsely; sprinkle **½ c grated parmesan** on top.

Spoon filling evenly over cheese. Gently arrange avocado slices in an even wagon wheel pattern around quiche. Set quiche on baking sheet; bake at 350° for 1 to 1¼ hours till light brown and beginning to puff up. Small cracks will begin to appear around the edges. It will fall slightly when you take it out to cool. Let it rest for at least 15 minutes before cutting to serve.

For pate brisee recipe, see page 119.

Use a serrated knife to cut. Cut from the edge toward the middle with the blade at about a 45 degree angle to the quiche. Use a very gentle touch.

Using the same pate brisee and batter, the chefs serve quiches with the following fillings:

Apple and Sausage

Brown 6 oz bulk seasoned sausage (according to taste). Drain, reserving ¼ cup fat. Peel and coarsely chop 2 medium green apples. Saute with ½ c sliced white onions, 2 cloves of garlic, minced, in reserved fat. Mix with sausage. (Note — sharp white cheddar or Fontina may be substituted for the parmesan.)

Ham, Feta, Black Olive

Use 1 c diced ham. Instead of parmesan, use 4 oz feta, ¼ c green onion, ½ c chopped black olives.

Snapper, Green Pepper, Pimento

Saute 6 to 8 oz baked and flaked snapper, ⅓ c medium diced green pepper, 2 to 3 pimentos, finely diced, ½ c diced green onions.

Serves 8.

For centuries before Europeans explored the Northwest there were rumors of a mighty river that emptied into the Pacific. The Spanish talked of the "River of Kings;" the English and Americans of a "Great River of the West." In 1792 the legends proved prophetic when Robert Gray discovered the mouth of the Columbia. The Columbia is truly a giant among rivers. It stretches over 1200 miles from the Canadian Rockies to the sea. By the time it reaches the Pacific it has drained one-fourteenth of the continental United States.

Greek Style Prawns

To saute can be a performance as well as a delicious way to prepare food. You can saute right at the table and serve immediately. In fact, you should saute immediately before serving, even if you do the work in another room. You need, however, to have all the ingredients prepared, measured and within easy reach. For this recipe, follow each step in order and without delay. Serve with Rice Pilaf.

flour
prawns
clarified butter
salt
white pepper
white onion
mushrooms
garlic
lemon
white wine
feta cheese
pernod
tomatoes
tomato sauce
green onions
parsley

Dust lightly in **flour 10 oz of prawns,** peeled and deveined. Heat ¼ **lb clarified butter;** add prawns. Brown on both sides.

Add **salt, white pepper to taste.** Immediately add **1 small white onion,** thinly sliced, **½ c mushrooms,** sliced, **1 to 2 cloves garlic,** minced, **juice of ½ lemon.**

Keep pan moving to keep flour from burning. Once ingredients are browned, add **¾ c white wine, 4 T feta cheese,** crumbled. Cook for a minute until cheese melts; add **½ c pernod.**

Add **8 small tomatoes,** diced, **4 T tomato sauce.** Keep stirring so cheese does not stick, but let ingredients marry for a few moments.

Add **4 green onions,** sliced thin, at the last moment. Remove to serve; garnish with **parsley.**

Serves 2.

Sauteed Prawns & Scallops

A delicate creamy affair with garlic that satisfies with its richness and fullness.

clarified butter	In large saute skillet (or 2 12" skillets), heat **3 oz clarified butter.** Add **8 16 to 20 size Mexican prawns (peeled and deveined), 4 to 5 oz 30 count scallops** lightly dusted in **1 c flour.** Bring heat to medium high. Season with **salt, white pepper to taste, squeeze of ½ lemon, 3 dashes tabasco.**
Mexican prawns	
scallops	
flour	
salt	
white pepper	Add **1 c sliced mushrooms** (½ c per pan), **½ c sliced onions** (¼ c per pan), agitating pan frequently to keep from burning the bottom. Turn ingredients; add **1 T minced garlic** per pan, **½ t chopped parsley** per pan.
lemon	
tabasco	
mushrooms	
white onion	
garlic	
parsley	Deglaze each pan with **2 T brandy, 2 T fish stock.** Let marry enough to incorporate ingredients; add **½ c heavy cream** per pan, **1 T grated parmesan** per pan. Bring together quickly; add **¼ c diced tomatoes** per pan, **2 small green onions,** sliced, per pan.
brandy	
fish stock*	
heavy cream	
parmesan	
tomatoes	If sauce is not reducing fast enough, remove scallops and prawns to prevent over-cooking and return sauce to high heat. Reduce to creamy consistency. Distribute vegetables evenly, lace sauce over.
green onions	
parmesan	
parsley	Garnish with **⅓ c loosely shredded parmesan** and **chopped parsley.**

For fish stock recipe, see page 182.

This is one of the recipes where advanced preparation is vital. Cooking time involves only 5 to 7 minutes; in electric heat you might extend to 10 to 12 minutes. Chef Lucas recommends that you clean the pans with a couple pieces of Italian Herb Bread.

Chef Lucas says, "If you're using fresh scallops, be sure to check for grit. Soak scallops in milk for 30 to 45 minutes to remove grit, and then strain through cheese cloth to free from debris. Often times you can incorporate liquid into sauce or plan a creative soup. Follow the flavors and it won't be as difficult as you think to make your own variation a table favorite. To waste the bounty is truly a violation!"

Serves 2.

Scallops with Prawns en Brochette

A gourmet delight from the grill with the flavor from the grill complementing the flavors from the marinade and the topping. In addition this recipe expands to accomodate extra guests. The flavors, the flexibility, the grilling — all make this an excellent choice for a relaxed outdoor dinner.

scallops
prawns
olive oil
garlic
parsley
lemon
salt
pepper
bib, leaf, or
butter lettuce
butter
pesto*
lemon
cherry tomato

Marinate approximately **3 scallops** and **3 prawns** per person in mixture of **1 to 2 T olive oil, ¼ t garlic, ¼ t parsley, juice of ½ lemon, salt, pepper to taste.**

Grill briefly on skewer; do not over cook these seafoods.*

Remove to **bed of finely chopped bib, leaf, or butter lettuce.** Top with mixture of **2 t softened butter** and **1 T pesto.**

Serve with **lemon wedge** and **split cherry tomato** as garnish.

For pesto recipe, see p. 170.

Depending on the heat of your coals, this should cook for 1 to 2 minutes. Test for doneness by squeezing.

Variations: add sliced white onion, mushroom caps, cherry tomatoes (at end). Try salmon on the skewer if available.

Recipe is per serving: multiply as needed.

Sake Scallops

Chef Lucas likes cooking with scallops partly because their texture is so smooth when prepared well and partly because they pick up so well the flavors of her striking sauces.

scallops

clarified butter

garlic

ginger

lemon

mushrooms

sake

teriyaki sauce*

bell pepper

tomatoes

orange zest

parsley

Saute **4 oz scallops** in **clarified butter;** add **¼ t garlic,** minced, **¼ t chopped fresh ginger.** Add a **squeeze of lemon, ⅓ c sliced mushrooms.** Deglaze with **¼ c sake.** Reduce, adding **4 T teriyaki sauce.** If need be, remove scallops from sauce as it reduces. Scallops must not cook for more than 4 minutes. At end, add **3 slivers bell pepper, ¼ c fresh chopped tomatoes.** Garnish with **orange zest** and a **sprig of parsley.**

For teriyaki sauce, process 4 t fresh garlic with ½ t fresh ginger. Add 1 c soy, ⅔ c sherry, juice of 2 lemons, ½ c brown sugar, 2 to 3 T honey. Blend.

Remember to be prepared before you start cooking because temperature and time are vital to the quality of scallops.

Recipe is per serving: multiply as needed.

Scallops Italian

Nanci has gone into her phone booth and changed from the baker's whites into a hostess dress to greet you at the door. Jimella and Robin get ready to prepare your entree while coordinating the appetizers and entrees as Carol gets the salads and breads together.

Last night, Mitzi, fresh from Washington State University where she studied Home Economics, sold bakery goods while preparing the genache and buttercreams for today's desserts. This morning, Mark, with Nanci, prepared your bread for this evening, as well as cookies, cakes, tarts and muffins. Tomorrow he returns to tend his property in The Dalles, Oregon, two hundred miles away, as he does two days each week. Yesterday Shelby drove the truck down the coast to pick up the fish and produce for your evening meal and returned to the restaurant to become the bookkeeper.

Robin, a Russian major in college, dodges back and forth along the cooking line with Jimella. Theresa — whom Nanci dubbed "Hot Shot" — flies back and forth between the dish washer and the appetizer table and back. It's a miracle that they don't all end up on the floor in a heap. But they don't; instead they coordinate to produce your Scallops Italian.

clarified butter
Oregon or Bay scallops
flour
mushrooms
shallots
lemon
tabasco
salt
white pepper

Heat **6 oz clarified butter** in skillet. Pat dry **1½ lb fresh Oregon scallops or East coast (bay) scallops** and dredge lightly in **flour.** Put into heated butter, scallops, **2 c sliced mushrooms, 2 t shallots,** minced, **juice of ½ lemon, 4 dashes tabasco, salt and white pepper to taste.**

When scallops are heated on one side, turn and add **2 t minced garlic, fresh chopped parsley, 6 oz fish stock.** Let blend a moment; add **¾ c fresh diced tomatoes, ½ c green onions,** sliced thin. Blend.

garlic
parsley
fish stock
fresh tomatoes
green onions
seasoned bread crumbs*
parmesan

Remove to individual casseroles or one casserole (scallops should be underdone to allow time to finish cooking in oven). Sprinkle **seasoned bread crumbs** generously over the top (makes a crisp, crusty top); sprinkle with **grated fresh parmesan.** Place in 450⁰ oven, top rack, for 5 to 6 minutes until top is starting to brown and liquid starts to bubble around sides of casserole.

For seasoned bread crumbs recipe, see page 26.

If using frozen scallops, remove to refrigerator and allow to thaw properly. (Remove as early as a full day before you intend to use them. In doing so they retain their juices.)

To prepare scallops soak them in milk for one hour. You can also use salt and cold water. If you use milk, run it through a cheese cloth to remove debris. The milk will have a wonderful scallop flavor, and in other recipes it acts as a sauce when tightened with roux.

Serves 4.

Chicken & Scallops with Tarragon

You want to be sure to let your guests take the first bite of this dish. It would be a shame for you to miss the look on their faces as they had their first taste of the stunning, but subtle blend of flavors here. It serves beautifully with Acini.

This recipe is per serving; simply multiply.

chicken breast
clarified butter
salt
white pepper
tabasco
lemon
tarragon
garlic
shallots
mushrooms
chicken stock*
white wine
scallops
heavy cream
parmesan
seasoned bread crumbs*

Cut each **4 oz chicken breast** into 2 pieces. Brown **1 T clarified butter:** 2 minutes on first side and just long enough on second side to seal. Season with **salt and white pepper to taste.** Add **dash tabasco, squeeze of lemon wedge.**

Add **¼ t fresh or dried tarragon, 1 to 2 cloves garlic,** minced, **¼ t shallots,** minced, **⅓ c sliced mushrooms.** Keep stirring or keep pan moving to prevent ingredients from sticking.

Add **1 oz chicken stock.** Deglaze pan with **¼ c white wine.** Add **4 to 6 scallops,** depending on size, **¼ c heavy cream, 1 T fresh parmesan.**

Let ingredients come together about 1 to 2 minutes, enough to blend thoroughly.*

Place sauce, chicken, scallops in casserrole, sprinkle top with **seasoned bread crumbs;** place **freshly grated parmesan cheese** on top.

Bake in 425⁰ oven till it starts to bubble — 8 to 10 minutes.

Do the bread crumbs first and set them aside. See page 26 for recipe.

For chicken stock recipe see page 183.

The butter measure is approximate; use no less than 1 T for two and no more than 3 T—that's how much you'd use for four servings. Do no more than four servings per pan.

You might wish to remove the chicken and scallops while you reduce the sauce until it reaches the degree of creaminess that you want.

On busy holidays sunbathers and waders sometimes went to the aid of swimmers beyond the breakers off Long Beach. Volunteers formed a human chain from the edge of the surf to the distressed bather and if the linked hands didn't separate, the bather could be brought safely ashore.

Chicken Dijonnaise

Serve this dish with either rice pilaf or with pasta; it's a whole new flavor for chicken, an exquisite mixture of complementary flavors.

clarified butter
chicken breasts
flour
yellow onion
mushrooms
garlic
artichoke hearts
dijon mustard
white wine
heavy cream
parsley

Heat **10 oz clarified butter** in saute skillet.* Lightly dredge in **flour, 4 6 to 7 oz chicken breasts,** boned; lightly brown chicken in butter, about 2 to 3 minutes.

When you turn to brown second side, quickly add ½ **c thinly sliced yellow onion, ½ c sliced mushrooms, 2 cloves garlic,** minced, **4 artichoke hearts.** Let vegetables heat in residue, but keep agitating pan to prevent garlic from burning. Add **2 oz dijon mustard, ¾ to 1 c white wine or cooking sauterne;** continue to move pan to blend mustard and wine well. Let liquid reduce by half.

As chicken comes ready, add ½ **c heavy cream.** Marry well and cook 3 to 4 more minutes to a creamy consistency.*
Remove the breasts to serving dish. Lace sauce over; sprinkle with **chopped parsley.**

It is really important to have all preparation work done before even heating the butter so you can move quickly to assemble ingredients.

Chef Lucas prefers a saute skillet with a rounded bottom and lip.

If chicken cooks faster than the sauce reduces, remove the chicken, keeping it warm, and raise the heat till the sauce is creamy; if the liquid reduces too quickly, add more wine, but no more than ¼ cup.

Serves 4.

Chicken Mediterranean

THE ARK serves this dish with acini, but if acini is unavailable, fettucine does beautifully. Be sure to coordinate the pasta preparation with the chicken, a simple matter: simply cook the acini or fettucine before starting on the chicken. Hold it in a strainer or colander until you need it.

clarified butter
flour
chicken breasts
shallots
parsley
garlic
oregano
mushrooms
white wine
chicken stock
tomatoes
feta cheese
green onions

Heat **3 T clarified butter** in saute skillet and dredge lightly in **flour 4 6 to 7 oz chicken breasts,** boned. Brown chicken on both sides; add **2 small shallots,** minced, **¼ t parsley, 3 small cloves garlic,** minced, **1 t oregano, 1 c mushrooms,** sliced. Marry into pan residue.

Add **⅓ c white wine;** blend well by moving pan quickly and steadily. Once well blended, add **½ c chicken stock, ½ c fresh tomatoes,** diced, **3 T feta cheese,** crumbled. Keep moving pan or stir frequently to distribute cheese completely into sauce.*

Add **¼ c thinly sliced green onions,** just soon enough for them to blend through and soften a bit.
Once sauce is reduced to the point of being creamy, remove to plates and serve.

For acini recipe, see page 64.

As for all recipes, have all the preparation done ahead so you don't have to stop everything while you chop mushrooms or measure stock.

You may wish to remove chicken while sauce reduces.

Serves 4.

Any traveller or resident can tell you: the Pacific Northwest gets a lot of rain. The western slope of the Olympic Mountains, about 100 miles north of The Ark, is the wettest place in the continental U.S. The rain forest in the Hoh Valley gets up to 150 inches per year; Mt. Olympus gets up to 200 inches. When Lewis and Clark wintered at Fort Clatsop, just south of the mouth of the Columbia, they recorded only 12 days out of 106 in which there was no rain.

Marinated Lamb Chops with Rosemary Sauce

The three hallogen lights spaced about 30 paces apart and brightly illuminating the bay shore against the pitch dark blue sky create the illusion that the night water has frozen and covered itself with a soft inch of snow. The tops of the sea grass provide a grey brush texture; they are quiet, but vibrant. The whole scene invigorates you as you gaze out the window and helps to make your fall dinner feel as though you're eating it on top of a satisfying day's work out of doors. This is the night to have Marinated Lamb Chops in Rosemary Sauce.

lamb chops
salt
pepper
olive oil
lemon
rosemary
garlic
clarified butter
white wine
raspberry wine vinegar
shallots
bay leaf
bouillon
butter
parsley
cayenne
artichoke bottoms
madeira

Pat **salt, pepper to taste** into single **lamb chops.** Marinate in mixture of **1 c olive oil, juice of 1 lemon, ½ t whole rosemary, ½ t garlic,** minced. Let stand overnight or at least 2 hours.

To cook, heat **2 T clarified butter** in saute pan. Brown chop in saute pan. Brown chop quickly, 2 to 3 minutes on first side, 1 to 2 minutes on second side. Remove to warming plate.

In another pan, bring to boil **¾ c white wine, ¼ c red raspberry vinegar, ¼ t whole rosemary, 1 shallot,** finely chopped, **¼ bay leaf.**

Turn heat down to simmer; reduce.

Add **2 T meat glace or extract or good quality bouillon or marrow stock.** Reduce by ¼.

Remove from heat; cool to room temperature.* Whisk in **2 T softened butter, 2 t chopped parsley, 1 dash cayenne, salt, pepper to taste.** Set aside.

Saute **whole artichoke bottoms** in pan
meat was cooked in. Deglaze with ¼ **c
madeira.** When bottoms are heated, serve
each chop on top of 1 artichoke bottom. Top
with dollop of rosemary sauce.

In preparing sauce, be sure it has cooled to
same temperature as butter before adding butter or sauce will separate.

If sauce is thin, add 1 T butter.

Sauce is like a buerre blanc sauce.

The marinated chops could also be served
with a mint sauce of choice. Simply marinate,
saute and serve.

Recipe is per serving: multiply as needed.

Veal with Pine Nuts

Of course, of all land animals whose flesh is prized, veal is royal. Delicate, subtle, tender beyond words.

The following recipe will astonish you, for all the strong flavors, the sauce merges with the veal; it does not overwhelm it. Then the pine nuts crown the royal dish perfectly.

veal
flour
clarified butter
salt
pepper
mushrooms
shallots
garlic
parsley
pine nuts
raspberry wine vinegar
lemon
dijon mustard
madeira
cream
onion

Cut **5 oz veal** into petite fillets.* **Flour** fillets lightly. Saute quickly in **4 to 5 T clarified butter. Salt, pepper to taste.** Brown on both sides; remove to warming platter.

Add to pan **½ c mushrooms, ½ t shallots,** minced, **½ t garlic,** minced, **¼ t parsley,** chopped, **1 full T pine nuts.** Pour in **2 T raspberry wine vinegar** and **1 squeeze lemon.** Add **½ t dijon;** marry well. Deglaze with **¼ c madeira;** add **2 T cream.** Reduce till thickened.* Add **1 T finely chopped green onion.**

Pour over veal.

Pound the veal with the heel of your hand. Gentle but firm touch.

Keep a high heat for reducing the sauce; it won't take but a couple of minutes to reduce, so you won't even have to put the veal in the oven to warm.

Recipe is per serving: multiply as needed.

Tournedos with Green Peppercorns

Shelby in the office in her green sweat shirt going through the bills from the previous night. Mark kneading bread, punctuating the morning air with sharp pounding sounds. Jimella supervises preparation in the kitchen; Rose gently tosses oysters with loving hands through cracker meal. The service people arrive wearing their black skirts and white blouses. As they move through the back hall they move through the area where the aroma from the rosemary French bread in the bakery ovens meets the aroma from the fish stock simmering in the kitchen. The sun breaks through the heavy clouds as they carry their rain load to the east across the bay. Floors mopped. Carpets vacuumed. Tables set. In a very few moments THE ARK will welcome you to lunch. Today's special: tournedos with green peppercorns.

beef fillets	Sear* **2 3 oz fillets,** dusted lightly with **flour.** Brown both sides, adding **salt, pepper.** Add **½ c mushrooms, ½ t garlic,** minced, **½ t shallots,** minced, **1 t dijon mustard.** Marry well. Add **1 t green peppercorns.**
flour	
salt	
pepper	
mushrooms	
garlic	Deglaze with **⅓ c brandy, ⅓ c madeira.** Reduce to about ½. Add **1 T cream.** Reduce* further till sauce darkens to color of caramel. Lace over fillets.
shallots	
dijon mustard	
green peppercorns	Serve with rice.
brandy	
madeira	
cream	

Butter must be hot to seal meat.

When reducing sauce keep sauce bubbling well. Stir or shake occasionally.

Recipe is per serving: multiply as needed.

When the salmon business was at its height in the Nineteenth Century, three harvesting methods were used. Seining, learned from the Indians who had practiced it for centuries, involved men and horses standing knee-deep in the water; in 1926 nearly six million pounds of salmon were taken by the seiners. Most of Ilwaco's fishermen were gillnetters, a dangerous occupation in which many drowned; after a heavy storm the gillnets that washed in would be tangled with dead bodies. Then traps were introduced about 1880 and by 1900 approximately 500 traps were in use between Fort Canby and Point Ellice at the northern end of the present Astoria Bridge. Late in the last century there were bitter gillnet wars between the trappers and the gillnetters.

NOTES

Breads & Muffins

THE IRREGULAR, RAMBLING AND NEVER-GET-THERE RAILROAD

Sometimes it was called the "Delay, Linger, and Wait Railroad," from its amiable habit in the early days of stopping wherever a passenger wanted off and its willingness to go back for forgotten parcels, deliver messages, or catch a runaway horse. The nickname, "The Irregular, Rambling and Never-get-there Railroad," came from the initials of its original owner, the Ilwaco Railroad and Navigation Company. When the Oregon Railroad and Navigation Company bought the line, about 1900, the company's engineer who inspected it said, "Hmph! Clamshell Railroad!" and that name, too, stuck.

It may have been the only railroad in the world that ran by the tide. Steamboats on the river could get to the Ilwaco dock, where the line started, only at mid-flood. Consequently the train, which met the boats, had to move its departure time back fifty minutes a day for six days, then six hours forward. As summer visitors increased, so did the railroad's passengers; sometimes in the early part of this century, the little engines carried ten coaches and two baggage cars. In 1908 a new dock was built at Megler because the shifting sands at Ilwaco made the ship crossing from Astoria dangerous and unreliable. A tunnel was built under Fort Columbia and the tracks ran down what is now the main beach highway from Megler to Nahcotta until 1930, when automobiles made the train unprofitable. Some local residents protested its demise, but its then owner, Union Pacific, held the hearing on discontinuing service in Astoria, too far for many protesters to go. A wreath was hung on the engine for the last run of the train that had served the peninsula since 1889. The engines were scrapped for junk, but no passenger rolling stock ever left the area. Residents bought the coaches for $25 apiece; one of them can still be seen by the highway that was once a railroad bed.

Rosemary French Bread

The difference in the taste of this bread is delicate, but definite. It serves well with main courses and salads, too. Each bite brings a puff of rosemary flavor, rising from the taste of yeast bread, parmesan cheese and garlic.

yeast
water
dry milk
salt

Dissolve **1 oz yeast** or 2 packages active dry yeast in **2 c warm water** in mixing bowl until it bubbles and foams — about 5 to 10 minutes.

malt syrup
vegetable shortening
rosemary
olive oil
parmesan
garlic
all purpose flour
cornmeal

Stir in **1 T powdered (non-fat) dry milk,** add **4 t salt, 1 T malt syrup** (1 T sugar or 1 T dark corn syrup can substitute for malt syrup.), **1 T vegetable shortening, 1 T dried rosemary,** (chopped fine and soaked in **1 T olive oil**), **1 T parmesan cheese,** fresh grated, **1 clove garlic,** finely minced. Mix thoroughly. Add **7 to 7½ c all purpose flour,** turn onto a lightly floured board, knead for 10 minutes — until it is smooth and elastic. Dough should be stiff.

Cover dough with large plastic bag and allow to rise for 90 minutes.*

Punch down dough, let it rest for 5 minutes.

Divide into three even pieces and shape into rounds.

Let these rest for another 10 minutes. Flatten and shape rounds into oblong loaves, tapered at both ends. Place loaves on a baking sheet sprinkled with **cornmeal.**

Cover loaves and let rise until doubled, about 2 hours.

Slit loaves lengthwise, and put into 400° oven with a shallow pan of ice cubes on the bottom of the oven.*

Bake for about 25 minutes, or until crusts are golden brown and sound hollow when you tap them.

Clear dough from bag occasionally (dough gives off moisture as it rises).

Ice cubes in oven will create steam during baking to produce a crisp crust. (Instead of using ice cubes, spray the loaves with short bursts of water from a mister every 10 minutes or so.)

Oregon Blue Cheese Bread

Just to the right of the entrance of THE ARK, a window opens to the bakery, allowing the smells of Chef Main's breads to greet the guests as they arrive. The yeast dough, blue cheese combination of this bread makes a special aroma which promises a special taste. You will find that the bread more than fulfills this promise. You will certainly want to try the various ways of serving it listed at the end of the recipe; you will also enjoy thinking up your own.

yeast
water
sugar
unbleached
white flour
milk
sugar
salt
butter
onions
eggs
worcestershire
flour
oregon blue
cheese*
chives

Dissolve **2 oz yeast** in **1½ c 90° water.** Stir in **2 T sugar** and **1½ c unbleached white flour** until smooth. Let sit about 20 minutes until it bubbles.

Meanwhile scald **1 c milk,** pour over **2 T sugar, 1 T salt, 3 T butter, 2 T dried onions.**

When the milk mixture becomes lukewarm, add it to the sponge (the yeast mixture); add **1 or 2 eggs, 1 t worcestershire.**

Stir in **5 to 6 c flour, 2 oz coarsely crumbled Oregon blue cheese, 1 T chopped chives.**

Empty dough to a bed of **1 c flour** and knead till smooth.

Put in greased bowl and invert to oil top. Cover with plastic wrap and let rise for an hour.

When risen, punch and form into 3 loaves; put into greased pans or put three round loaves on flat pans. (Or, the recipe makes about 45 dinner rolls.)

Let rise for 45 minutes, covered.

10 minutes before putting in oven, score tops.

Brush with milk and bake at 350° for 35-45 minutes. (25 minutes for rolls.)

Brush tops with egg wash for a gloss. (Beat 1 egg and add 1 T water.)

To serve: of course, you'll love eating this bread plain: fresh and warm with sweet butter, but you can also use it for appetizers, toast it or make sandwiches. Treat yourself to a real surprise: try a grilled cheese sandwich with havarti cheese on blue cheese bread.

Roquefort or other blue cheese will do in place of Oregon blue; THE ARK uses only Oregon blue, of course.

Kümmel Bread

Chef Main developed this recipe in honor of her mother, a "thoroughbred Swede who loves this version of limpa bread." You don't have to be Swedish, however, to enjoy this thoroughly Swedish bread; all it takes is to taste it — you will become a temporary, honorary Swede, one with a big smile and a happy mouth. Eat it with spicy pates or sausage. It complements cheeses beautifully. Or simply toast it. *Tack sa mycket.*

kümmel liqueur
water
fennel
anise
caraway
orange peel
medium rye flour
butter
salt
yeast
brown sugar
white flour
molasses
orange peel
lemon peel
unbleached white flour
coffee

Boil for 5 minutes **1 c Kümmel liqueur, 2 c water, 2 T fennel, 2 T anise, 2 T caraway, 1 T orange peel.** (For a more moist and mellow bread, use 1½ c water with ½ c milk instead of 2 c water.)

Strain this liquid into **2 c medium rye flour, 2 T butter, 1 t salt** and stir to a thick paste. Cool to lukewarm.

Dissolve **2 oz cakes yeast** in **1 c water, 90°.**

Add **2 T brown sugar, ½ c white flour** and let this mixture rest 5 to 10 minutes till bubbles appear.

Add yeast mixture, **½ c molasses, 1 T grated orange peel, 2 t grated lemon peel** to the rye paste; knead in **5 to 6 c all-purpose unbleached white flour** until dough is smooth and elastic. Place dough in oiled bowl and invert the dough to coat. Cover dough with light plastic bag and let rise until doubled. (You can freeze the dough at this point. When you are ready to use it, simply thaw and follow the next steps.)

Punch dough down and form into 3 ¼ lb round loaves or 4 loaf pan loaves; let proof till doubled. Score halfway through the proofing.

Heat oven to 375°.

Bake loaves 30 to 45 minutes — until they sound hollow when tapped. About 10 minutes before they are done, brush the loaves with **¼ c strong coffee.**

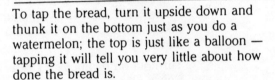

To tap the bread, turn it upside down and thunk it on the bottom just as you do a watermelon; the top is just like a balloon — tapping it will tell you very little about how done the bread is.

Pesto Bread Sticks

A rare and wonderful treat at THE ARK is the fried cheese marinara with pesto bread sticks on the side. Chef Nanci Main insists that the proper form is to dip the sticks in both the sauce and the cheese.

yeast
sugar
water
all-purpose flour
milk
butter
salt
pesto*
egg wash*

Dissolve **2 cakes yeast** and **2 T sugar** in **1½ c 90⁰ water.** Add **1½ c all-purpose flour.** Stir to thick paste, no lumps. Cover; let sponge rise 20 minutes.*

While sponge rises, scald **1 c milk;** add **3 T butter, 1 T salt.** Allow mixture to cool to lukewarm; add **3 T pesto, 4½ c all-purpose flour.** Mix.

Turn out on bed of **½ c flour.** Knead till firm. Cover; let rise 10 minutes.

Pat dough down. Cut in half; cut halves in half; continue halving until you have 32 pieces. Roll pieces out to sticks about 12 inches long. Lay on greased sheet pan. Cover.*

Let rise 15 minutes, till nearly doubled. Brush with **egg wash;** bake at 375⁰ for about 30 minutes — till lightly browned on top.*

See p. 170 for pesto recipe.

Use large mixing bowl from start.

For egg wash, beat 2 egg yolks, mix with 3 T milk.

You will also like pesto rolls made by tying dough sticks into pretzel knots, tucking ends underneath.

Carrot Raisin Bread

The orange flecks from the carrots in this slightly yellow bread set off the brown raisins. Meanwhile the flavors the spices produce blend with the yeast dough to treat your nose. But the moment of wonders is when you cut yourself a thick thick piece — about two inches — and spread with plenty of soft butter. Fresh out of the oven you have a reward for being present at this creation's arrival.

milk	Scald **1 c milk;** add **2 T sugar, 1 T salt, 1½ t butter.** Stir till melted. Cool to luke warm.
sugar	
salt	
butter	Add **1 egg,** beaten; blend thoroughly.
egg	Dissolve **1 cake yeast** in **1 c lukewarm water.** Add to above mixture. In separate bowl combine **6½ c all-purpose flour, 1½ c raisins, 1 t cinnamon, ½ t allspice, ¼ t ground cloves, ½ t nutmeg, 2 c ground carrots.**
yeast	
water	
all-purpose flour	
raisins	Add dry ingredients to liquid. Mix thoroughly. Turn out on lightly floured board. Knead about 10 minutes till smooth. (It will spring back to touch.)
cinnamon	
allspice	
cloves	
nutmeg	Put in lightly greased bowl; invert to grease top. Cover. Let rise 1½ hours — till doubled.
carrots	

Punch down; divide into three; place in greased pans; cover. Let rise 1 hour till doubled again.

Bake in 375⁰ oven 30 to 40 minutes till browned.

Date Nut Bread

Chef Main says "This recipe was given to me by my grand-mother. She came over from Sweden and she was a cook for many years here in the United States and she didn't even know English. When I got this recipe from her, it said 'butter the size of an egg.'" Well, she may have had some difficulty with English, but you will find that her date nut bread speaks a universal language.

water	Pour **2 c boiling water** over **1 c chopped**
dates	**dates** and **⅓ c butter.**
butter	Let rest till butter melts; cool to lukewarm.
eggs	Add **2 eggs,** well beaten (Be sure the mixture
vanilla	is not hot enough to cook eggs.) and **1 t**
sugar	**vanilla.** Mix.
baking soda	Mix **1½ c sugar, 2 t baking soda, pinch of**
salt	**salt, 3 c white all purpose flour,** and add
flour	to liquid ingredients. Stir in **1 c chopped**
walnuts	**walnuts.**

Put batter into 2 greased bread pans and bake at 325° for about 50 minutes or until a toothpick comes out dry.

Remove from oven, let cool in pans for 10 minutes. Remove to a rack.

Wrapped in foil, this bread slices and freezes beautifully; what it does even more beautifully is get served with whipped butter or even better yet, whipped cream cheese sprinkled with walnuts.

Pate Brisee

This recipe is given here to be prepared either by hand or by food processor. It makes a classic pastry crust.

pastry flour
salt
unsalted butter
egg
ice water

By hand: combine **1¾ c sifted pastry flour, ½ t salt** and make a well in the center. Cut in **4 oz unsalted butter** (cool), cut in small pieces, with fingers or a pastry blender. Blend in **1 egg yolk** and sufficient **ice water** (⅓ c or less) to make dough.

Wrap in cellophane and chill at least 1 hour before rolling. Grease a 10 x 2 deep dish quiche pan. Roll out dough and lay across pan letting it fall into place and gently forming dough into sides of pan. Leave ⅓ inch edge and fold in to form finished edge. Note: 2 shallow quiche pans may be substituted. Wrap and store in freezer.

By food processor: put flour, salt, butter in the bowl. Whirl it until butter is size of small peas. Quickly put in egg yolk and then ice water. As soon as dough begins to come together, stop processor. Mold remainder by hand. Wrap in cellophane, chill, and roll out as with the directions above.

Butterhorns

Chef Main says of this recipe, "A very special friend, Roberta Kerner, gave this recipe to me. Her Butter Horns were a standard treat on her family's fishing trips. The mace adds a nice subtle touch."

sugar
salt
mace
nutmeg
eggs
vanilla
lemon rind
shortening
milk
flour
yeast
butter
cinamon
walnuts

Cream together **⅓ c sugar, 1 T salt, ½ t mace, ½ t nutmeg, 3 eggs, 1 t vanilla, 1 t grated lemon rind, ⅓ c softened shortening.** Add **¾ c cold milk** and then **4 c chilled sifted flour** to above. Crumble **4 cakes compressed yeast** in **½ c cold milk** and add to mixture.

Mix in **2 c flour.**

Chill dough for 15 minutes. Turn out onto well-floured board. Roll dough into circle, making edges thin.

Spread **1¼ c soft butter** in center ⅓ of rolled out dough. Fold sides in, covering butter.

Turn dough over and roll into rectangle. Fold into thirds (like a business letter) and roll again in opposite direction. Repeat 3 times, chilling about ½ hour between each rolling out.

Cover and let rise 30 minutes.

Roll dough into sheet 15 inches wide. Sprinkle with **cinnamon** and **sugar.** Fold in thirds so it is 5 inches wide. Cut in strips and let stand 5 minutes.

Twist by holding one end in left hand and roll away from you with right hand. Twist in circle towards you and make tighter roll. Fasten in center by pinching. Turn over and place on lined or well-greased baking sheets. Brush with glaze made of ¼ **c milk** and **1 egg.**

Let rise 1 hour.

Bake at 450⁰ for 15-18 minutes or till done. Cool slightly and frost while still warm.* Sprinkle with chopped walnuts. Serve warm with pat of butter.

For frosting, combine 2 c sifted powdered sugar, 2 T softened butter, 1 t vanilla, enough milk to make thick glaze.

Makes 18 to 24.

Wheat-Germ Muffins

The most difficult part of this recipe is that it takes three separate bowls.

brown sugar
butter
flour
baking powder
salt
buttermilk
egg
baking soda
wheat germ
raisins*

Heat oven to 400°; grease muffin tins.

Bowl one: combine **1 c brown sugar, ¼ c soft butter.**

Bowl two: combine **1 c all-purpose white flour, 2 t baking powder, ½ t salt.**

Bowl three: combine **1 c buttermilk, 1 egg, 1 t baking soda.**

Add in **1 c wheat germ** and **1 c raisins,** stirring as little as possible.

Add contents of bowls one & two to bowl three.

Put batter into greased tins and bake for 18 to 20 minutes.

Golden raisins do well, as do the more traditional variety.

Variations: Add 1 t of finely grated orange peel or ½ t cinnamon or ½ t nutmeg.

Makes 18 to 24.

Honey Bran Muffins

Lunch at THE ARK. Watching the oyster boats and crab boats coming back in. You are relaxing with a cup of coffee. Then comes the serving person with a basket of these muffins and a dish of cranberry butter. They are, of course, served warm, made fresh that morning by Chef Main. When you take your first bite, you know you have come home no matter where you hail from.

buttermilk
honey
butter
eggs
brown sugar
cake flour
baking soda
bran
salt
nutmeg
dates

Preheat the oven to 400°.*

Combine **2 c buttermilk, ½ c honey, ¾ c melted butter, 3 eggs, 2 c packed brown sugar.** Whisk until they dissolve together.

Stir in mixing bowl **3 c cake flour, 2 T baking soda, 3 c bran, 1 t salt, ½ t freshly grated nutmeg.**

Make a well in center and add liquid mixture all at once. Stir about 10 seconds until incorporated, then sprinkle the **½ c chopped dates** over the mixture and finish mixing.

Spoon batter into lined muffin tins until ¾ full and bake them 20 to 25 minutes at 400°.*

The oven must be 400° or the muffins will sink. Do not over mix after adding dates, or texture will be grainy and tough. Stir briefly.

Variations: Add 1 T grated orange peel instead of the nutmeg or use raisins instead of dates. Also you can add ½ c chopped walnuts.

Makes 18 to 24.

Good food is not new to the North Beach Peninsula. In the late Nineteenth Century, vacationing campers could, for 25ᶜ, eat a complete dinner at the Baker farm on Sand Ridge Road. One of Mrs. Baker's specialties was a cream dessert made from seaweed gathered at China Beach near Ilwaco. Called "moss fareen," the moss was black when it was picked but turned lavendar, pink, or white after it was dried and moistened. When Mrs. Baker stirred it into milk, the milk thickened and could be molded — good with whipped cream on top.

NOTES

Desserts

BERRIES

Wild berries have always been abundant on the Long Beach Peninsula. Flat orange salmon berries line the roadsides and volunteer themselves in the yards of gardeners who are less than ruthless. This berry may have been named for its color, but James Swan suggested, in his 1857 account of life on Shoalwater Bay, that the name might have come from the berries ripening in June, with the first salmon run, or from their beneficial effects on the digestion of Indians who had eaten too much rich salmon too fast. Wild red strawberries abound on the dunes, too tiny for any but the most patient. When the railroad ran down the peninsula, a favorite pastime was gathering the wild red huckleberries, no bigger than currents, that grew along the right-of-way. The black salal berries, which grow on tough bushes in the woods and along the cliffs — the rocks below North Head are covered with them — are not much used by white people; they were, however, a staple food of the Indians, cooked, fresh, or dried.

Most important commercially are the cranberries, but although nowadays they are cultivated in well-tended bogs, they too were once wild. Very small native cranberries grew on fine, hairy vines; Lewis and Clark had them for Thanksgiving dinner in Chinook in 1805. Cultivated vines were brought from New England in the 1880's and planted in the bogs on Cranberry Road, where the Quinault Indians, who always knew just when to come without being told, harvested them by hand. Now the cranberry crop, a major product of the peninsula, is gathered by vacuum machines.

Strawberries & Cream Mousse

This mousse is more assertive than most mousses; the fresh fruit is really evident in the flavor as well as in the texture. If fresh berries are not available, you can use frozen — the texture, of course, will not be quite the same. You'll still love it.

gelatin
strawberry juice
cream cheese
sugar
strawberries
whipping cream
vanilla
framboise syrup*
red currant jelly

Dissolve **1 T gelatin** in ¼ **c strawberry juice.** Set aside. In mixer, whip **8 oz softened cream cheese** till fluffy, scraping bowl often. With lumps gone, slowly add ½ **c sugar,** beating at medium speed. Add **1 c pureed strawberries;** mix well. Add strawberry juice-gelatin mixture in steady stream, continuing on medium speed.

Fold in **1 c coarsely chopped strawberries.**

In separate bowl, whip 1¼ **c whipping cream** till holds soft peaks. Add ½ **t vanilla, 1 T framboise syrup.**

Fold whipped cream into strawberry mixture, reserving small amount for garnish. Transfer to serving glasses. Pipe a whipped cream rosette on each mousse.

Reduce **1 c red currant jelly** over low heat until thickened slightly. Dip perfect **whole strawberries,** one at a time into the jelly, hold a few seconds to give glaze a chance to set, place gently, one on each rosette.

Framboise syrup is available in import and specialty stores — also at gelato stands.

Raspberries are wonderful as are wild blackberries. With the latter, use Grand Marnier instead of framboise.

A striking variation is apples and blackberries. Puree the apples, mix with chopped black-berries, use blackberry juice and rum.

Serves 6.

Caramelo

This is one of the most popular and decadent desserts served at THE ARK. Its combination of chewy caramel custard with smooth whipped cream and crunchy nuts will remind you of a candy bar, but no candy bar ever tasted like this. It's wonderful with coffee. This recipe makes six servings.

sweetened condensed milk

evaporated milk

genache*

pound cake

liqueur

whipping cream

powdered sugar

liqueur or rum

filberts

Combine **1 c sweetened condensed milk, 1½ c evaporated milk** in 2 quart heavy bottomed saucepan;* bring mixture to boil, stirring constantly. Reduce heat to low; continue cooking mixture, stirring constantly, for 30 to 40 minutes until mixture reduces to thick custard and turns pale beige. (The mixture will have a temperature of about 200º.) At this point, you will have about 1¼ cups custard.

Remove custard from heat; cool for 10 minutes. Divide mixture in half; stir **3 generous T genache** (2 oz melted unsweetened chocolate can be substituted) into one half of it. When mixtures have cooled completely, put a **small piece of liqueur soaked cake** into each serving glass. Spoon equal parts of plain caramelo and chocolate caramelo over cake.

Whip **1 c whipping cream** with **1 T sifted
powdered sugar** and **1 T liqueur of
choice or rum** and pipe over individual
caramelos. Garnish with sprinkle of **chopped
filberts.**

Don't use an aluminum pan since it may
discolor the caramelo.

See page 138 for Genache recipe.

You can add ¼ cup melted peanut butter to
the vanilla portion while still warm and top
with coarsely chopped peanuts.

Dark rum, Amaretto, or Grand Marnier are
Chef Main's favorites with Caramelo.

Serves 6.

Chocolate Peanut Butter Pie

Rich flavored as you'd expect, but surprisingly light and smooth;this ranks as one the favorites at THE ARK. You'll be surprised how easily it all goes together.

graham crackers	Crust
chocolate wafers	In one bowl, combine **¾ c crushed graham crackers, ¾ c crushed chocolate wafers, ¼ c sugar, ¼ t cinnamon, ⅛ t mace, ⅛ t fresh ground nutmeg, ¼ c coarsely crushed sliced almonds** (crush sliced almonds coarsely by hand if you like).
sugar	
cinnamon	
mace	
nutmeg	In another bowl, combine **¼ c melted butter, 1 T dark rum, 1 T vanilla.** Mix two combinations.
almonds	
butter	
dark rum	Line 9 inch pie plate with 1½ c to 1¾ c of crust mixture.*
vanilla*	
cream cheese	Filling
sugar	Whip **8 oz softened cream cheese** until fluffy, scraping bowl often. Slowly add **1 c sugar, 1 c creamy peanut butter, 2 T melted butter.** Whip **1 c whipping cream** and **1 T vanilla** until firm.
creamy peanut butter	
butter	
whippping cream	Blend ⅓ of whipped cream into peanut butter mixture.
vanilla	Fold peanut butter mixture into remaining whipped cream until thoroughly incorporated.
	Fill pie crust, smoothing top.
	Chill.

*semi-sweet
chocolate
butter
salad oil
peanuts*

Topping

Combine **4 oz semi-sweet chocolate, 2 T butter, 2 T salad oil** in top of double boiler until chocolate melts. Cool slightly.

Spread chocolate mixture on cooled peanut butter filling, starting from center and working out.

Sprinkle top with **¼ c chopped peanuts.** Chill pie thoroughly.

The extra pie crust mixture has many wonderful uses: use it for cheesecake crust, sprinkle it over mousse as garnish, fold it into whipped cream to fill a cake. To save it, simply freeze in an airtight bag.

Mexican vanilla will add a special touch.

Use a hot dry knife to cut twelve portions per pie.

Garnish each piece with whipped cream.

Serves 10 to 12.

Swedish Cream

After a heavy meal, you'll find this light, smooth sour cream custard just the right touch. You might even be able to convince yourself that it is low calorie because it has yogurt in it. After one bite, though, it won't matter.

water
gelatin
heavy cream
sugar
plain yogurt
sour cream
vanilla
Grand Marnier
Cranberry Grand Marnier Sauce*

Soften **2 t gelatin** in **1 T cold water** in saucepan. When soft, add **1½ c heavy cream, ½ c sugar.** Put pan on medium heat, stirring constantly with spoon until gelatin dissolves; make sure you reach to pan's corners. Do not allow mixture to boil. Remove from heat and transfer to bowl.

Let cool — about 20 minutes — stirring occasionally. Fold in **¼ c plain yogurt, ¾ c sour cream, ½ t vanilla** (Mexican, if possible), **2 T Grand Marnier.**

Pour into 6 serving glasses or parfait glasses; cover with plastic wrap and refrigerate for about an hour.

Top each dessert with **1 to 2 T Cranberry Grand Marnier Sauce** (and rosette of whipped cream.)

See page 166 for Cranberry Grand Marnier Sauce recipe.

A mixture of blackberries, lemon peel and Amaretto or Grand Marnier makes a nice alternate topping.

Raspberries also accent Swedish Cream well.

Serves 6.

Bruceport, a once thriving oyster town on the east side of Willapa Bay, took its name from a ship, the Robert Bruce, which was set afire by a mutinous crew in the bay. Since the crew had no ship to leave the area in, they went on shore and settled there.

Chocolate Cranberry Torte

This delicious cake, a concoction of chocolate, cranberries, French buttercream, and whipped cream, is one of the delights that may arrive on the dessert tray after a dinner at THE ARK. It takes some time and planning to prepare, but the reward of the first bite speaks for itself.

You should make the cake first, then the genache, then the chocolate French buttercream, and finally the simple syrup and the whipped cream filling.

Genache*

heavy cream	In saucepan combine **2 c heavy cream, 2 oz**
butter	**butter, 2 oz sugar.** Bring mixture to boil.
sugar	Remove from heat; add **1 lb slivered semi-**
semi-sweet	**sweet chocolate.** Stir till melted. Cool to
chocolate	room temperature, cover; refrigerate.

Chocolate French Buttercream

sugar	Combine **2 c sugar, 2 T glucose, ½ c**
*glucose**	**water** in 2 quart sauce pan. Beat **4 eggs** till
water	frothy while bringing sugar mixture to a boil,
eggs	using pastry brush to wash down sides of pan
cold unsalted butter	with water. When mixture reaches 235⁰ or soft
	ball stage, slowly add to eggs in thin stream,
genache	mixer on high. Continue to beat on high until
vanilla	cool. Reduce speed to medium and slowly add
	1¼ lbs cold unsalted butter cut into small
	chunks. As you add chunks one at a time, the
	mixture will look curdled but it will eventually
	smooth out. Add **2 c genache** and **1 t**
	vanilla.

Buttercream freezes well. Thaw and beat till smooth but don't overbeat or you will get too much air in the buttercream and it won't spread as smoothly.

If buttercream gets too soft, refrigerate till firm again.

In place of genache, 8 oz melted semi-sweet chocolate may be substituted.

Cake

cocoa
butter
espresso
coffee
flour
baking soda
salt
sugar
buttermilk
eggs
vanilla
cranberries

Preheat oven to 375°. Grease and flour 3 8" pans or 2 9" pans.

Melt ¾ **c cocoa** and **6 oz butter** in ½ c **espresso** and ½ **c coffee.** (You may use 1 c strong coffee in place of the espresso/coffee mixture.) Sift together **2 c all-purpose flour, 1½ t baking soda, ½ t salt, 2 c sugar.** Pour chocolate mixture into bowl and stir in dry mixture; still beating, slowly add ½ **c buttermilk.** Next add **2 eggs,** beaten; **1 t vanilla.** Fold ¾ **c coarsely chopped cranberries** into the mixture. (Chop cranberries while frozen for cleaner cut.) Pour the batter into pans; bake for 25 minutes.

Cool cakes for 10 minutes; remove from pans. Cool to room temperature. Wrap in plastic and freeze.

Simple Syrup

water
sugar
framboise*

Heat **½ c sugar, ½ c water** in pan until sugar completely dissolves. Remove from heat; stir in **2 T framboise syrup.**

Whipped Cream Filling

whipping
cream
powdered
sugar
framboise

Whip **¾ c cream** till thickened. Add **2 T powdered sugar** and **1 T raspberry syrup.**

Assembly

chocolate curls
cranberries

Split layers of cake in half lengthwise. You will use four layers in the torte. (The extras can be wrapped in plastic and frozen.)

Lightly brush each with simple syrup.

Place one layer of cake on serving plate. Spread top with French Chocolate Buttercream.

Place second layer on top. Pipe a ring of French Chocolate Buttercream around outside edge. Fill in center with whipped cream filling.

Top with third layer. Frost with Buttercream.

Put fourth layer on top. Frost completely with Buttercream.

Garnish torte with **chocolate curls** and **cranberries.**

Genache is the stuff truffles are made of! Use the best quality chocolate.

Framboise syrup is an imported raspberry syrup.

Corn syrup may be substituted for glucose.

Paul Bunyan, the mythic logging hero, is credited in folk tales with carving the geography of the Northwest. When (as the story goes) Paul thought his trusty blue ox, Babe, was dying, he scooped out a huge grave near the Pacific. The giant logger threw the rocks and dirt to side as he dug the grave. Babe recovered, to Paul's great joy. Paul then dug a huge channel to the ocean and the unused grave was filled with water. Today the channel is the Juan de Fuca Strait; the unused grave is Puget Sound; the heaps of stone and dirt are the Cascade and Olympic mountain ranges that straddle the Sound.

Frangelico Gateau

Evening at THE ARK. Nanci watches the clumsy white clouds bumbling along, filling the horizon to the north toward the mouth of the Willapa. Customers stop to chat about her Rosemary French Bread and her Swedish Cream. One of the customers can barely contain himself: "And that Gateau — the Frangelico. I just couldn't believe it. Where did you find that recipe?" Nanci pauses a moment. "It developed over the years. I'm glad you liked it."

And now you can like it in your home. The recipe is a bit elaborate, calling for a bit of time, a bit of planning and a loving touch. But don't serve it just for special occasions — serving it makes a rainy Tuesday special. If you prepare the genoise and the buttercream ahead of time, you cut down the preparation considerably.

It comes in steps: Hazelnut Genoise, French Buttercream, simple syrup and flavored whipped cream.

eggs

superfine sugar

cake flour

filberts

unsalted butter

vanilla

gelatin

water

whipping cream

powdered sugar

frangelico liqueur

simple syrup*

french buttercream*

Hazelnut Genoise

In a large metal bowl, warm **6 eggs** and **1 c superfine sugar** to 100°. It will appear dark yellow and syrupy.

Beat the eggs until pale yellow and until a ribbon forms when beater is lifted — about 7 to 10 minutes.

Combine **1 c sifted cake flour** and ½ c **finely ground toasted filberts.** Lightly fold into eggs using a lifting motion from sides of bowl to center. Fold in ½ c **unsalted butter,** clarified, and **1 t vanilla.**

Pour into 2 9 inch greased cake pans, lightly floured.

Bake until sides just begin to pull in — about 20 to 30 minutes at 350⁰. Let them rest in pans for 10 minutes. Remove and let cool to room temperature. Wrap gently in plastic wrap and freeze.

Whipped Cream

Soften **1 t gelatin** in **1 T cool water.** Dissolve over hot water. Whip **1 c whipping cream** at medium speed until thickened. Still beating, add **3 T powdered sugar** and then gelatin mixture. (Be certain to add gelatin in a continual motion so it doesn't lump up.)

Add **3 T Frangelico, ¼ t vanilla;** beat till firm, not dry.

Assembly

Remove genoise from freezer and gently split them into two thinner rounds. Gently brush **simple syrup** on first layer using patting motion and flat side of brush.

Spread **buttercream** over first layer — about ¼ inch thick. Set second layer on; brush top with simple syrup.

Pipe buttercream in ¼ inch border around outside of layer. Spread inside with whipped cream.

Set third layer on. Brush with simple syrup. Spread with ¼ inch layer buttercream.

Set final layer on top. Refrigerate till firm.

Gently trim sides making straight, even sides. Frost top and side with buttercream.

Refrigerate till firm.

For the French buttercream recipe see p. 138. But instead of genache, substitute ¼ t almond and 2 T frangelico for flavoring.

For simple syrup recipe see p. 140. But instead of Framboise substitute 2 t frangelico for flavoring.

You may freeze this cake; thaw well ahead of serving time in refrigerator; about 10 to 15 minutes before serving, set at room temperature.

Presentation suggestions: use decorating comb on sides; put filbert in center of piped rosettes on top of gateau. Pipe border around top and fill center with whipped cream swirls; sprinkle with finely chopped toasted filberts. Finish with white chocolate filigree decorations fanning out from center.

Serves 10 to 12.

Apple-Pear Tatin Parfait

If you have Creme Fraiche on hand, this recipe becomes one of the easiest and quickest elegantly rich desserts you have ever tried. It's a perfect dessert for a summer or warm fall afternoon.

Creme Fraiche*

heavy cream
buttermilk

Stir **1 T buttermilk** into **1 c heavy cream.** Put bowl in oven overnight. (Heat from oven light will be enough to thicken it.) When thickened refrigerate.

Apple Pear Tatin

apples
pears
butter
sugar
nutmeg

Peel, core, quarter **3 pears** and **5 apples.** Melt **4 oz butter** with **1 c sugar** in heavy skillet. Add fruit and stir until coated. Let mixture come to boil, reduce heat to simmer. After 30 minutes, pour off 1 c juice and reserve. Let mixture simmer 30 minutes longer, stirring occasionally to coat fruit. Remove fruit from skillet, add reserved juice and simmer 10 minutes until thickened and golden. Pour over fruit.

To serve, layer in 6 parfait glasses: three layers with creme fraiche in center and fruit mixture on top and bottom. Garnish top with dollop of creme fraiche and grating of fresh **nutmeg.**

Creme fraiche will keep 2 weeks refrigerated.

Creme fraiche can be whipped up like whipped cream.

Serves 6.

Chocolate Amaretto Cream

You'll be delighted with the delicate flavor of this dessert; you'll be amazed at how easy it is to prepare.

Cream

gelatin
water
heavy cream
sugar
semi-sweet chocolate
sour cream
amaretto liqueur

In saucepan, soften **2 t gelatin** in **2 T water.** Add **1½ c heavy cream, ½ c sugar, 2 oz semi-sweet chocolate,** shredded. Stir over low heat until sugar and gelatin dissolve completely and chocolate completely melts, about 5 minutes.

Set mixture aside; cool until lukewarm, stirring occasionally. Whisk in **1 c sour cream,** and **3 T Amaretto liqueur.** Pour into 6 serving glasses leaving space for topping. Cover each with plastic wrap. Refrigerate for 6 hours or overnight.

Topping

whipping cream
confectioner's sugar
amaretto liqueur

Whip **¾ c whipping cream** in large bowl to consistency of thick custard. Fold in **3 T confectioners sugar, 2 t Amaretto liqueur.** Refrigerate until ready to serve, 1 to 3 hours. At serving time, simply spoon topping on individual creams.

Garnish with macaroons or toasted almonds.

Serves 6.

Old Fashioned Bread Pudding

Chef Nanci Main has taken this traditional dessert and changed it to an exquisite dessert, retaining the essense of the older versions while transforming it into an extraordinarily delicate treat.

bread crumbs

half and half

vanilla

egg yolks

sugar

butter

Bread Pudding

Butter 3 quart baking dish. Soak **2 c soft French bread crumbs** in **1 qt half and half,** room temperature; add **1 T vanilla** (Mexican is best.)Place **5 egg yolks** in mixing bowl; set mixing bowl in pan of hot water. Stir yolks constantly till warm and dark yellow.* Remove mixing bowl from hot water and beat yolks at high speed until pale yellow. Lower speed to medium; gradually add **1 c sugar.**

When sugar is mixed in, add **1 T melted butter.** Put speed on low; add ⅓ bread crumb mixture. (Scrape bowl regularly so it all incorporates into mixture.)

Blend in remaining bread crumb mixture; mix thoroughly. Turn into buttered baking dish; bake at 350⁰ for 45 minutes or until set. (The edges will begin to pull from sides.) Remove from oven and top with meringue.

Meringue*

egg whites
salt

Set the oven at 450⁰ as soon as you remove the pudding.

cream of tartar
sugar
fruit
nutmeg

Beat **5 egg whites** with a **pinch of salt** until foamy. Add ¼ **t cream of tartar** and beat until large bubbles become smaller. Gradually add ½ **c sugar,** beating until stiff but not dry. Spread meringue on top of pudding right to the edges (either use a spatula or pipe a design with large star tip).

Place in oven until meringue colors.

Assembly

Serve warm or cold with fresh **fruit** (blueberries, strawberries, peaches, raspberries, brandied fruit, or stewed apples with a bit of chutney) and rosettes of whipped cream piped on top with freshly grated **nutmeg.**

To stir the yolks for the pudding, use a whip, or better yet, your hands, because you have to take care that the heat doesn't cook the yolks and your hands work better to keep track of the temperature.

Another interesting topping: simmer fresh cranberries with sugar, orange rind, and then combine with walnuts and mandarin oranges.

Flavor the whipped cream with rum, amaretto, grand marnier or raspberry juice.

Lemon curd sauce is a time honored topping for bread pudding. For lemon curd recipe, see page 168.

THE ARK customers are presented with this favorite dessert in tulip glasses on a doily. You can top the pudding with the fruit before applying the meringue, or else top with the fruit and pour heavy cream around the edge of the pudding , topping with a bit of meringue.

Serves 10 to 12.

Until a very few years ago visitors who climbed up on the North Jetty on Long Beach could watch the Columbia River Lightship moving back and forth at the entrance to the river. It kept the weather records for the area. Ironically, when it was replaced by computers, storms knocked out the new system and records for several weeks were lost. Nevertheless, the lightship didn't return. It's now moored at the Maritime Museum in Astoria, Oregon, for the edification of the curious.

Tapioca Zabaglione Custard

Perhaps some June evening you will hit it lucky: a warm day on the beach, clouds occasionally keeping the edge off the heat, perhaps a little rain to wash everything off, and dinner at THE ARK.

Now the dessert tray arrives and your luck has held: in the middle of the tray, surrounded by all the other wonderous dishes from Chef Main sits a dish of Tapioca Zabaglione Custard. Topped with fresh raspberries and a puff of whipped cream. You must be living right. A perfect day.

small pearl tapioca
water
half and half
salt
marsala
eggs
egg yolks
sugar
vanilla
raspberries
whipped cream

Soak **⅓ c small pearl tapioca** in **¾ c water** overnight. Drain and combine with **2½ c half and half, ¼ t salt** in heavy bottomed pan. Bring to boil, stirring constantly with whip. Reduce heat; simmer 20 minutes, stirring often. Add **½ c marsala;** simmer 25 minutes, still stirring often. Remove from heat; stir in **1 c half and half** slowly. Combine **2 eggs, 2 egg yolks, ½ c sugar.*** Stirring constantly, add ⅓ cream mixture to egg mixture; add back to remaining cream mixture still stirring constantly.

Return to low heat for 5 minutes — Do Not
Boil. Remove; add **½ t vanilla.** Stir till
thoroughly mixed.

Dish into dessert glasses; cool.

Top with fresh unsweetened **raspberries** and
whipped cream rosette.

Set bowl with egg mixture on a wet towel
and it won't tip when you stir in cream mixture.

Variations: strawberries, peaches, blueberries,
blackberries. Remember: don't sweeten fruit;
the custard will complement the natural ripe
tartness of the fruit.

Use old fashioned small pearl tapioca — not
instant. (Large pearl could be used.)

This dessert is best served on same day it's
made.

Serves 6.

Creamy Raspberry Cheese Cake

Sunday evening at the ARK in the summer changes your soul. At 5:30 the sun has lost its heat (it's about 60⁰) but not its brilliance. It goes down on the west side of the peninsula while the moon comes up from the east. The bay waters pull at you, deep blue water patched with bright green sea grass lying between you and the dark green fir trees on Long Island. In the distance grey green hills hover beyond Shoalwater Bay. Puffy white clouds cast shadows over the tide as it does its miracle rising to cover the exposed bottom of the bay shore. A sea gull floats overhead on the breezes while its mate sits on the grey boat beached right outside your window. And everything is hushed. A glass of the featured Washington wine, fried Brie Cheese in Marinara Sauce appetizer with Pesto Bread Sticks, an entree, and dessert — Creamy Raspberry Cheese Cake to finish off your summer Sunday evening meal at THE ARK.

cream cheese
sugar
flour
eggs
vanilla
grand marnier
orange rind
raspberries
almonds
sour cream
whipped cream

Beat **2 lbs softened cream cheese** till light, scraping bowl often. Add **1¾ c sugar** slowly. With mixer still running, add **1 T flour,** then **4 eggs,** one at a time followed by **½ t vanilla** and **2 T Grand Marnier.**

Remove from mixer and add **1½ t finely grated orange rind** and gently fold in **1 c raspberries.** Coat inside of lightly buttered 10 inch spring-form cheese cake pan with **finely ground almonds.** Pour batter into pan; set pan on sheet of tin foil. Pull foil up around and above sides of pan and fold into collar. Set in pan with in ½ inch boiling water; bake at 325⁰ for 1¼ to 1½ hours — until set. (Cover with foil if it starts to brown.)

Remove foil collar, let rest 10 minutes. Make topping by mixing **3½ T sugar** and **1 t vanilla** into **1 c sour cream.** Pour topping over cheese cake and return to 325⁰ oven for 10 minutes. Cool. Chill at least 3 hours, preferably overnight.

Just before serving, Chef Main covers sides with **thinly sliced almonds** and garnishes each piece with a **raspberry** set in a **whipped cream rosette.**

Cut with dry hot knife; wipe blade after each cut and run hot water over blade periodically to keep it hot.

Serves 10 to 12.

Wild Blackberry Tart

This blackberry tart is really wild.

flour
salt
butter
cream cheese
sugar
eggs
lemon rind
vanilla
blackberries
corn starch
sugar
lemon juice

Crust

Combine **1 c flour, pinch of salt** in food processor. Cut into small pieces **8 T butter, 6 T** (3 oz) **cream cheese**; distribute pieces over flour. Process till dough just begins to come together. (Do not overwork dough.) Form into ball by hand. Wrap in plastic and refrigerate for ½ hour.

Roll out on lightly floured surface. Carefully lay in 9 inch or 10 inch lightly greased tart pan.(Do not stretch dough. Patch rather than re-roll. Again: dough will become tough if you work it too much.) Trim edges leaving ½ inch finished edge. Freeze for 1 hour.

Parbake (bake, but not all the way through) 15 minutes to set crust. Do not bake through. Pierce any bubbles that start to form while baking — before bubbles can harden.

Filling

Whip **12 oz softened cream cheese** thoroughly till all lumps are gone. Scrape sides of bowl often. Put mixer on low; add ½ **c sugar** slowly, scraping bowl often. Add **2 eggs,** one at a time. Mix in **1 t grated lemon rind, ½ t vanilla.**

Pour into crust; bake in 350⁰ oven till lightly puffed and set. It should just be on the verge of starting to take on a light golden hue — do not overcook — about 30 minutes. Cool at room temperature about ½ hour.

Topping

Mash **1 c wild blackberries;** strain; reserve pulp. Add **3 T corn starch to juice;** mix thoroughly. Add **1 c sugar.** Put over medium heat; stir until it becomes translucent and thickened — about 2 minutes. Boil until thickened and slightly reduced. Remove from heat. Add **reserved pulp** and **3 c wild blackberries, 1 t lemon juice,** freshly squeezed. Stir. Spread gently over tart. Rest at room temperature 30 minutes; refrigerate till firm.

Cut with clean, hot, dry serrated knife. This will keep the dark berry color separate from the rich white cream filling.

Serves 10 to 12.

Strawberry Marzipan Tart

Chef Main remembers Kathy, a friend from the bay area in California, who gave her the recipe for this crust. Actually Kathy Lattin uses this dough to make hundreds of holiday butter cookies. "Kathy makes the cookies and invites her friends over to decorate them. Then when you go to her place, she shows you all the cookies and tells you who decorated which ones." Chef Main thus has a special kind of feeling for this recipe and uses the dough to make a special crust for Oregon strawberries — so special themselves with their deep red color all the way through, matching perfectly their deep lush flavor.

all-purpose flour
salt
baking powder
butter
sugar
eggs
vanilla
milk
almond paste
lemon rind
apricot jam
strawberries
currant jelly

Crust

Sift together **2½ c all-purpose flour, ¼ t salt, 2 t baking powder.** Cream **½ c softened butter;** slowly add **1 c sugar.**

Add **2 eggs,** one at a time, scraping sides of bowl after adding each egg. Add **½ t vanilla.** Slowly add dry ingredients and **1 T milk.** Chill for 1 hour.

Roll out on lightly floured board and place gently in greased 12 inch tart pan. Pat into place about ¼ inch thick.

Franganpani

Soften **8 oz almond paste** in mixer. Slowly add **3 T sugar** and **6 T softened butter.** Scrape bowl. Add **3 eggs,** one at a time. Beat until just incorporated; do not over beat. Add **3 T flour, ½ t finely grated lemon rind,** taking care to keep sides of bowl scraped.

Assembly

Spread **3 T apricot jam** across crust bottom.
Spread Franganpani over jam, sealing edges.
Bake at 350⁰ for approximately 30 minutes until light golden.

Wash, hull, gently dry **whole strawberries.***
Invert strawberries across entire top of tart.*
Heat **1 c currant jelly;** simmer till slightly thickened, use pastry brush to dab glaze on strawberries and spaces between.

Dry strawberries by rolling gently across dry towel.

Trimming berries to same size will enhance the presentation.

Left over dough can be frozen. It can also be baked in bars for cookies — brush with melted chocolate and sprinkle with nuts.

Serves 10 to 12.

White Satin Tart

If just saying the name of this dessert doesn't convince you to try it, run your eyes over the list of ingredients. It's a dead heat between calling it satin or silk. No matter what it's called, the flavor will convince you to have it often.

You prepare it in four easy stages.

tart crust	Prepare the crust described on p.154 . Bake till done, about 30 minutes at 350º.
raspberries	
sugar	Glaze
corn starch	Puree **½ c fresh raspberries;** strain. Add
white chocolate	**1 T sugar,** stir. Dissolve **1 t corn starch** in the puree. Bring to boil; let the mixture thicken. Let it cool; spread over baked crust.
butter	
eggs	Filling
semi-sweet chocolate	Melt **4 oz shredded white chocolate** in bowl over hot water bath. Whip **½ c softened butter;** gradually add **⅔ c sugar.** Beat till incorporated — till pale yellow. With beaters at minimum speed, add white chocolate in steady stream. Scrape bowl constantly. Do not allow chocolate to harden on side of bowl. Add **1 egg;** turn mixer to high. Beat 3 minutes. Add **1 more egg;** beat three more minutes (again scrape bowl sides constantly). Pour filling to center of crust to allow it to spread to sides on its own. Smooth carefully from center to sides.
vegetable oil	

Topping

Melt **2 oz semi-sweet chocolate** in hot water bath with **1 t butter.** Add **1 t vegetable oil.** Mix well. Drizzle fine lined spiral circle on top of tart. Refrigerate till firm.

Pull blade of knife lightly over top from center to edges making a spider web effect. Be sure to wipe knife after each pass to insure a clear design.

Refrigerate.

Serves 10 to 12.

Na-ko-ti was a Chinook Indian who lived just south of the present Nahcotta wharf. He invited R. H. Espy and I. A. Clark, the founders of Oysterville, to look at the oysters on his side of the bay. When they were lost on the water in a heavy fog, Na-ko-ti guided them in by thumping his Indian drum. He knew who they were, he said, because they splashed their oars too much; Indians could row silently.

On what used to be called "the weather beach," a couple of miles across the peninsula from Nahcotta, the three-masted French schooner Alice *ran aground in 1909. Until 1930 the last of her masts showed above the water, and the remnants of her hull could be seen at low tide until 1950. Although the Alice was for years a famous landmark, she was only one of the more than 150 ships that perished between the mouth of Willapa Bay and Cannon Beach, Oregon, since records have been kept. The official list records only vessels of more than 25 tons; the smaller ships that met disaster are too many to count.*

NOTES

Stocks & Sauces

BEACONS TO THE SEA

In the early days the only aids to mariners trying to get into the Columbia River were three tall firs with their tops slashed, occasionally bonfires at night, and sometimes a white flag in daylight. Then in 1856, after two years of difficulty, during which one of the supply boats itself went aground on the sands, Cape Disappointment lighthouse was finished. It was equipped with a Fresnel lantern, built in France in 1822 and used in New England for thirty years. The lantern used 130 gallons of sperm oil a month in five wicks and could be seen for 21 miles at sea.

When North Head lighthouse was built in 1898, the old Fresnel lantern was moved there. Both beacons were completely automated in 1937; the old lens and the lighthouse keepers were retired; huge electric lenses provide timed signal beams and the Coast Guard gives the occasional inspections that are needed.

Cape Disappointment is the oldest standing lighthouse in the Pacific Northwest and the highest on the Washington Coast. North Head is the windiest light on the Pacific, perhaps in the world. And the old Fresnel lantern, all its hundreds of glass prisms gleaming, is on display at the new Lewis and Clark Interpretive Center that clings to the cliffs above Fort Canby. The glass has a chip or two where a wild duck, dazed by the light, went through a heavy window pane in 1932 and damaged the prisms a bit. Neverthless, the lantern still justifies what a relative of Robert Louis Stevenson said long ago: "I know of no work of art more beautiful or creditable to the boldness, ardor, intelligence and the zeal of the artist."

Cranberry-Grand Marnier Sauce

cranberries
water
sugar
grand marnier
orange

Bring to boil **2 c water** with **1 lb fresh or frozen cranberries** and **2 c sugar;** let simmer until skins begin to pop open, about 10 minutes. Run through food mill or a food processor. Strain. Be sure to push pulp through strainer.

Add **¼ c grand marnier** and **1 t grated orange peel.**

This will make about 2 c cranberry sauce; if this seems like too much, the recipe can be cut in half. It freezes extremely well.

This sauce makes the ideal finishing touch for Swedish Cream and for Salmon Lucas, but it also makes an unusual, delicious topping for French Vanilla ice cream. Put it on the ice cream hot for a real treat.

Cranberry Butter

Wait till you put this butter on warm honey bran muffins; it will bring back that wonderful Sunday brunch by Willapa Bay — or if you haven't been there yet, look at the picture on page 67 while you put the first bites in your mouth. Then simply keep your eyes closed for the rest of the muffin. You are at THE ARK.

butter
cranberries
brown sugar
honey
walnuts
cranberry sauce
orange peel
lemon peel
buttermilk

Whip **1 lb softened butter** at high speed until it's pale yellow, scraping the sides of the bowl to make sure all the butter gets whipped.

Add **½ c raw cranberries,** coarsely chopped (if they are frozen, chop them while they are frozen and let them thaw before starting), **¼ c brown sugar, ¼ c honey, 4 T ground walnuts, ½ c cranberry sauce, 1 T grated orange peel, 1 t grated lemon peel.** Whip at medium speed until light pink.

Add **2 T buttermilk** and whip until incorporated.

You may freeze this butter and re-whip it when you want — simply thaw and add 1 T buttermilk.

Single portions can be molded and frozen; just thaw them when it's time to serve.

The sweet tartness lends itself to waffles, pancakes and french toast, as well as muffins and sweet breads.

Lemon Curd

Lemon curd makes a superb warm sauce over bread pudding and chilled it is a perfect topping for toast. The smooth consistency and tart flavor will inspire you to uncover a good many other uses.

corn starch
sugar
water
egg yolk
butter
lemon rind
lemon juice
golden raisins

Combine **1 T cornstarch, 3 T sugar** in saucepan. Add **1 c cold water** and stir in with a whisk until mixture is incorporated and all lumps are out.

Put over heat. Simmer till transparent.

Remove from heat and stir ⅓ of the hot mixture into **1 beaten egg yolk** in a bowl. Once that is mixed well, put it back into pan and incorporate two mixtures and return pan to heat for a minute or two, until sauce thickens up — but don't let it boil.

Remove from heat and stir in **1 t butter, 1 T lemon rind, juice of 1 lemon, 2 T golden raisins.** (Butter will melt and raisins will soften with heat.)

Watercress Sauce

This unusual, sharp sauce complements smoked salmon pate perfectly. Like many dishes at THE ARK, it strikes you with its unique and perfectly balanced blend of flavors.

watercress

dijon mustard

salt

black pepper

vegetable oil

lemon juice

evaporated milk or sour cream

Puree **1 oz watercress, 2 T dijon mustard.** Add **1 t salt, freshly ground black pepper.**

With machine running, drizzle **1 c oil** slowly as mixture thickens.

Add **2 t lemon juice.** Stir in.

Add **1 to 4 T evaporated milk** or **sour cream** while machine continues to run.

Pesto Sauce

A wonderful sauce with many uses. Be sure to try the quick and wonderful Sole with Pesto that is so easy to prepare. Keep many small packages in your freezer — ready to use at a moment's notice. Make plenty when basil is in season and you'll be happy the rest of the year round.

basil*
parsley*
garlic
pine nuts
salt
parmesan
olive oil

Put in a food processor and blend well

5 c firmly packed and cleaned fresh basil, ¼ c chopped parsley, 9 cloves garlic, minced, **½ c pine nuts, 1 t salt, ½ c fresh grated parmesan cheese.**

Add **¾ c olive oil** in a small stream, slowly, with machine running. Continue to blend until it is a smooth green paste.

Be sure to use fresh basil; dried basil does not produce the same intensely flavored pesto sauce.

Use Italian flat leaf parsley if possible.

To freeze, use an air tight plastic container. Put ½ inch or so of olive oil on the top of the sauce to seal it.

Pesto is a versatile sauce: great not only on sole but also with steamed clams, salmon, vegetables. Mix it with cream cheese and spread on canapes or cream it with butter and spread on fresh warm bread. Or serve on pasta.

 Tartar Sauce

Perhaps, like so many, you like tartar sauce — let's say with deep fried perch — but you don't like to admit it. Here's a solution: make this version of what is a classic sauce, and when you serve it on, for example, the Halibut du Chef, everyone will know that tartar sauce has been brought to new heights without losing its old charm.

green pepper

celery

onions

parsley

kosher dill pickles

worcestershire

lemons

tabasco

salt and black pepper

garlic

mayonaise

In food processor, grind **1 small green pepper, 4 large ribs of celery, 2 medium small onions, 5 healthy sized sprigs of parsley** (no stems, just the tops). Strain in china cap (or fine wire mesh); let stand until they lose most of their juices.*

Grind **5 large whole kosher dill pickles** in processor.* When vegetables are drained, mix with ground pickles, juice and all.

Stir vegetable and pickle mixture into **1 qt mayonnaise** and add to mixture **1 T worchestershire sauce, juice of 3 lemons, 4 dashes tabasco, salt and black pepper to taste, 2 cloves garlic,** minced. Make sure ingredients are well incorporated.

The combination of the ground vegetables will often times have a bitter effect on the sauce if you don't drain them.

For best results, this sauce should be made in advance to allow the flavors to mature (even overnight).

The juice from grinding the pickles gives this sauce a distinctive flavor that complements the flavor of fish beautifully.

Tomato Sauce

You will want to prepare this ahead of time, when fresh tomatoes are in season. It refrigerates well and also freezes easily.

butter
onion
thyme
basil
oregano
garlic
tomatoes
white wine

Melt **2 T butter** in sauce pan, saute
½ medium onion, diced, until just clear. Add
a **pinch of thyme, basil, oregano,**
3 cloves garlic, minced. After a moment,
add **6 medium tomatoes,** diced (4 c canned
Italian plum tomatoes may be substituted),
¾ c white wine (Sauterne or Chablis according to your preferences).

Stirring frequently, bring mixture to rolling boil.

Reduce heat, simmer about 30 minutes.

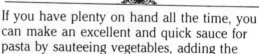

If you have plenty on hand all the time, you can make an excellent and quick sauce for pasta by sauteeing vegetables, adding the sauce and pouring over pasta.

Hollandaise Sauce

This is Chef Lucas' own version of the classic sauce; make a full recipe and keep it on hand in the refrigerator.

egg yolks
tabasco
salt
white pepper
worcestershire
white wine
clarified butter
lemon
ice water*

Put **4 egg yolks** in the top of a double boiler and while heating, whisk vigorously with **1 dash tabasco, salt** and **white pepper** to taste, **1 dash worcestershire, 2 T white wine.**

When you see the marks from the whisk and it has turned pale yellow, turn heat off and add slowly **¾ c to 1 c clarified butter,** a bit above room temperature.

Continue to whisk until it reaches the right consistency. Add the **juice of ½ lemon** and serve.

Keep the ice water handy; if the sauce starts to break, add drops of the water. Keep the water level down in bottom half of double boiler. Keep a cotton towel between the steam and the bowl.

Barbeque Sauce

You'd never suspect that a hearty old favorite could become this kind of taste experience. Those who taste it for the first time get wide eyes, moan quietly and eat till they can no longer focus their eyes at all. Veterans just eat and eat and eat.

tomato sauce
tomato ketchup
liquid smoke
white vinegar
tabasco
onion
prepared mustard
garlic
brown sugar

Combine in a large pot and mix well,
**3 c tomato sauce, 3 c tomato ketchup,
½ c liquid smoke, 2 c white vinegar,
1 T tabasco, 1 small onion,** diced fine,
**3 T prepared mustard, 3 large cloves
garlic,** minced, **1½ c brown sugar.**

Bring mixture to rolling boil over high heat, stirring frequently from bottom to keep onions and garlic from settling to the bottom and scorching. When it boils, turn heat down and simmer 1 to 1½ hours.

Take from heat; cool at room temperature. Once cooled, cover and refrigerate. It will keep well for up to a month if covered properly and refrigerated.

Serve this sauce with oysters in the shell or with prawns in a casserole. Oysters, fresh shucked and topped with this sauce and then with parmesan cheese, are wonderful.

Another idea for serving: spread the sauce lightly on 6-8 oz salmon fillets in a baking dish and bake for about 12 minutes in a 425° oven.

Wonderful on sliced beef or chicken for quick lunch sandwiches.

Cut French bread, spread the sauce on it, add Double Gloucester or Leicester cheese and toast/broil from the top.

Or put poached egg on bread or English muffin, spread sauce over the egg, add grated cheddar cheese, top with jalapeno slices and toast/broil till the cheese melts. Serve with chilled fruit for a perfect breakfast.

Aioli Sauce

Aioli sauce makes a spectacular addition to bouillabaisse or cioppino; simply add a generous dollop to each bowl. It is quick and easy to prepare and refrigerates well.

milk
garlic
red raspberry vinegar
eggs
salt
white pepper
olive oil
lemon
heavy cream

Combine **3 T milk, 4 large cloves of garlic,** minced, **2 T red raspberry vinegar, 2 egg yolks, ½ t salt, ¼ t white pepper.** Place mixture in blender or food processor; blend until mixture is thick.

Add **⅓ c olive oil** drop by drop while machine is running.

Add **¾ c olive oil** in a thin stream.

Quickly add **2 T lemon juice** and **1 to 2 T heavy cream.**

Be sure you have all the ingredients measured and ready to use before you start.

It also makes an unusual and subtle dip with cruditees, cooked vegetables or provencale fish.

 Garlic Butter

The recipe shows preparation methods for hand or food processor.

mushrooms
garlic
scallions
unsalted butter
brandy
sherry

By hand: mix ¼ **c mushrooms,** chopped, **3 large cloves garlic,** chopped fine, **2 whole scallions,** chopped fine, ¼ **lb unsalted butter,** softened. Blend thoroughly.

By food processor: use metal blade. Chop mushrooms, add garlic, scallions, softened butter.

Add **2 T brandy, 2 T sherry** and blend.

This yields ½ cup. It will refrigerate well so keep some on hand for other uses. Just keep it covered in the refrigerator.

Roquefort Dressing

Roquefort — the royalty of salad ingredients. Unfortunately, few recipes for dressings that use this unique cheese measure up to it. This is one. It's relatively simple, as you can see, but in addition, it not only keeps well, it actually matures — it gets better as it refrigerates. If you have some in your refrigerator, you will soon find yourself using it as a dip for fresh vegetables as well.

celery

onions

parsley

sour cream

horseradish

lemon juice

worcestershire

tabasco

black pepper

salt

garlic

raspberry wine vinegar

roquefort

blue cheese

mayonnaise

buttermilk

beer

Grind **4 ribs of celery, 2 small onions, 6 full sprigs of parsley.** Let drain in a china cap (a conical shaped strainer) or a fine wire mesh strainer.*

Add **2 c sour cream, ½ c horseradish, ½ c lemon juice, 2 T worcestershire, 3 shakes tabasco, ¼ t black pepper, ¼ t salt, ½ t garlic,** minced, **½ c raspberry wine vinegar.** Stir.

Grate into the mixture **¾ lb roquefort ¼ lb blue cheese.** (The blue cheese adds a lovely sharp flavor to the subtleness of the roquefort.) Stir till mixed well.

Add **3 c mayonnaise, ½ c buttermilk, ½ c beer.** Mix.

It's important to drain the ground vegetables because the combination of juices, if left to sit, produces a bitter aftertaste.

Let it stand for at least a couple of hours to let the cheese flavors establish themselves.

To store, simply cover well and keep in the refrigerator.

For a great sandwich, spread roquefort dressing on turkey and rye bread sandwiches.

Use this dressing in an omelet and add sauteed mushrooms and onions if you like.

At a potlach teams of eaters often climbed into the food containers to eat as much as possible. At The Ark frequent visits might prove a more effective (and aesthetic) way to sample the many tempting dishes.

Vinaigrette Dressing

This is a wonderful sauce for tossed salad; it is unbelievable with calamari.

sugar

olive oil

red raspberry
wine vinegar

salt

black pepper

lemon

parsley

garlic

Mix a **pinch of sugar, 10 T olive oil, 2 T red raspberry wine vinegar, salt, fresh ground black pepper, 1 T fresh lemon juice, 1 T chopped fresh parsley, at least 1 T minced fresh garlic.** Store in a covered container in the refrigerator.

For a fascinating variation, try walnut oil instead of olive oil.

Some special uses: marinate whole button mushrooms, or artichoke hearts, or green onions, or fresh tomatoes. Serve with calamari bodies and tentacles which have been submerged in boiling salted water for 30 to 35 seconds. Put calamari on a bed of lettuce and dribble vinaigrette over so some gets on the lettuce.

Italian Dressing

Given Chef Lucas' heritage, her fondness for Italian dressing comes as no surprise. Her own version of the classic Italian dressing is a creamy vinaigrette. If you have a jar of it in your refrigerator all the time, you are in the enviable position of being a few lettuce-washing minutes away from the best salad you can have away from THE ARK.

garlic
green onions
parsley
dijon mustard
pepper
lemons
red raspberry wine vinegar
olive oil
vegetable salad oil
sugar

Blend well in a food processor **8 cloves garlic, 2 green onions,** sliced, **1 t chopped parsley, 1 T dijon mustard, 3 twists of a peppermill, juice of 2 lemons, 3 T raspberry wine vinegar.**

With machine running, slowly add **1 c olive oil, 1 c vegetable salad oil.** Add **1 t sugar** to take the sharpness off the garlic.

Fish Stock

As you prepare fish, especially salmon and snapper, freeze the scraps until you have about a pound; then make stock. This way six cups of fish stock is virtually free. When the stock is prepared, freeze it in the smallest quantities you are likely to use it, about 1 cup per package.

fish scraps*
onion
bay leaves
water
carrots

Put in pot and bring to a rolling boil **1 lb fish scraps, 1 onion** (Just cut the onion in half; leave the skin on.), **2 medium sized bay leaves, 2 qt cold water, 2 carrots,** cut in chunks. Lower heat, cover and simmer about 3 hours. Remove from heat, strain, store.

Salmon and snapper are best; halibut can be added in small quantities. You can also use whitefish. For scraps use heads **without the gills** (very important: remove the gills), tails, bones and trimmings.

Chicken Stock

Using the gizzards in this stock adds the gelatinous quality to the stock that can't be achieved otherwise.

*chicken necks
and backs
gizzards
onion
whole cloves
thyme
whole
peppercorns
carrots
parsley
water
salt*

In an 8 quart pot, add **2 to 3 lbs chicken parts** and **2 lbs gizzards, 1 onion** stuck with **whole cloves, 1 t whole thyme, 6 peppercorns, 2 carrots,** cut in chunks, stems and tops of **1 c parsley.** Add **3 to 4 quarts cold water.** Bring slowly to a boil, skimming scum which forms on the surface.

Add **salt** to taste. Cover and simmer 1 to 1½ hours. Taste for seasoning and let simmer another hour. Strain through cheese cloth and let cool thoroughly. Remove fat.

beef bones
onions
salt and pepper
red wine
carrots
celery
parsley
bay leaves
peppercorns
thyme
water

Heat oven to 500° about 10 minutes before you put bones in. Put **5 to 6 lbs of beef bones** (knuckle or good prime marrow bone) on a sheet pan or a baking pan in a 500° oven for 40 minutes. (The bones will spew and spit and stink up your kitchen; don't be alarmed.)

During the first 20 minutes, move bones around on pan to guarantee full cooking.

Skin and cut up **3 onions** and lay them over bones after bones have cooked for 40 minutes. Sprinkle **salt** and **black pepper** over bones and onions; bake for 50 minutes.

After bones have baked for an hour and a half, remove from oven; lift bones and onions from pan with spatula or slotted spoon. (Dump out grease from pan, but don't scrape pan; you will be using what's stuck to the bottom.)

Put baking pan on top of stove and pour on **3 to 4 c red wine** (water may be substituted). Heat mixture to loosen juices, etc., stuck to bottom of pan.

Put liquid and bones into stock pot.

Cut into chunks **2 carrots** and **1 small bunch celery** (wash the celery and then cut it up, leaf, stalk, root and all). Add **roots of 1 small bunch parsley, 1 onion quartered** (skin and all), **3 bay leaves, 1 T black peppercorns, 3 sprigs fresh thyme** (or 1 T dried whole thyme).

Add enough water to stock pot to cover bones by at least 2 to 3 inches.

Put pot on burner leaving lid off. Bring to high boil, adjust heat to maintain constantly rumbling boil. Cook for a minimum of 4 to 6 hours (8 to 24 hours is even better). As stock cooks, keep replenishing water to maintain the 2 inches of water over bones.

After the stock is cooked, strain it. (A china cap or a fine wire mesh strainer is fine. It's not necessary to strain through cheese cloth if you're using this for onion soup base because a sturdier stock works well.)

*rom the
eastern windows of the
Ark, diners can look
across the bay to Long
Island, which seems to
be covered entirely with
pine and Douglas fir.
What now appears
uninhabited — and it is,
at least by human be-
ings — was in the
1870's the site of Dia-
mond City, a town of
75 people. Named not
for jewels but for
something that was
then almost as valuable
— the white oyster
shells on which the set-
ting sun glittered like
diamonds — the village
disappeared with one
of its main reasons for
existence, the native
oyster beds.*

NOTES

Index...&c

ALL I EVER WANTED WAS TO FISH

"My family has been fishing for two hundred years," Ernie said as he started his boat away from the Nahcotta dock to check his crab pots. "That's all I ever wanted to do, but it's getting harder and harder to make a living."

Ernie goes out alone to tend his 105 pots, strung out on lines from Nahcotta to the mouth of Willapa Bay. He builds his own pots, almost all of them, round wire structures that weight fifty pounds or more empty. He baits the traps with discarded oysters from the Nahcotta plant and with other discarded shellfish, the latter a carefully guarded secret that accounts for his getting more crabs from fewer pots than other crabbers on the bay. He is meticulous about abiding by the regulations. He throws back every female, every crab whose shell hasn't hardened, and every crab less than the required six and a quarter inches across the back, as measured by his calipers. He resents the fishermen that keep illegal crabs; he wants crabbing to endure, he says, so that his sons can go out in crab boats when they grow up.

He has reconstructed his own boat. He repairs his own engine and mends his own lines. But in spite of all his energy and all his strenuous work, he's finding it hard to make ends meet. One day's run down the bay, a six-hour trip, garnered enough legal crabs to fill about two standard garbage cans. It's not enough.

Ernie is too young to remember the time, forty or fifty years ago, when almost anybody could find a crab hole on the beach at low tide and pull Dungeness crab out with a blunt-tined rake. But he knows about it, and he knows the crab are getting scarcer, like everything else that has been over-harvested.

LIST OF TERMS

Clarified Butter — The oil from the butter; the fat has been removed. Since the fat burns at a lower temperature than the oil, you can saute much hotter with clarified butter. See page 25, for how to clarify butter.

Deglaze — When you saute, a certain amount of residue sticks to the pan. Adding wine or liqueur pulls the residue up and allows it to marry well with other sauce ingredients.

Garlic — Not only an excellent food to lower blood pressure, a foolproof method of fighting off vampires, but a simply beautiful food. Use it often and with imagination.

Heavy Cream — Whipping cream, commercially. If possible, use cream without lots of additives. Sometimes it's not possible.

Marry — A lovely term. This is what happens as sauce ingredients merge, blend, come together — marry.

Parbake — Bake a shell ½ way. The surfaces are baked, the inside requires further baking.

Proof — Proofing dough is letting the dough rise. This is what makes your kitchen smell so nice.

Roux — A paste made with butter and flour. Added to sauces, it thickens them. For recipe, see page 26.

Water Bath — To bake pates or cheese cakes, you put terrine or cake pan into a larger pan with boiling water at least ½ of the way up the side of the terrine or pan. If you use a spring form pan, be sure to wrap in tin foil, so it is water proof. You don't want water in your cheese cake.

SUGGESTIONS FOR FURTHER READING

Some of the information in the vignettes and historical sketches, and a great deal more, can be found in

Bancroft-Hunt, N. and Werner Forman. *People of the Totem.* Orbis Publishers, London, 1979.

Chinook Observer Centennial Edition. January 1, 1981.

Clark, Ella E. *Indian Legends of the Pacific Northwest.* University of California Press, 1953.

Davis, Edgar and Charlotte. *They Remembered.* Privately printed, 1981.

Drucker, Philip. *Cultures of the North Pacific Coast.* Harper & Row, 1965.

Florin, Lambert. *Washington Ghost Towns.* Superior Publishing Co., 1970.

Gibbs, James A., Jr. *Pacific Graveyard.* Binfords and Mort, 1950.

Gibbs, James., Jr. *Sentinels of the North Pacific.* Binfords and Mort, 1955.

Gibbs, Jim. *West Coast Lighthouse.* Superior Publishing Co., Seattle, 1974.

The Great Northwest. Weathervane Books, N.Y., 1978.

Holbrook, Stewart H. *Far Corner, a Personal View of the Northwest.* Macmillan, 1952.

McDonald, Lucile. *Coast Country.* Binfords and Mort, 1966.

Mills, Randall V. *Railroads Down the Valleys.* Pacific Books, Palo Alto, 1950.

Mills, Randall V. *Steam-wheelers up Columbia.*
Pacific Books, 1947.

Morgan, Murray. *The Last Wilderness.* Viking
Press, N.Y., 1955.

Phillips, James W. *Washington State Place
Names.* University of Washington Press, 1971.

Shaw, Frederic *et al. Oil Lamps and Iron
Ponies, a Chronicle of the Narrow Gauges.*
Bay Books Ltd., 1949.

Swan, James G. *The Northwest Coast or Three
Years' Residence in Washington Territory.*
Harper, 1857; University of Washington
Press, 1972.

Thwaits, Reuben G. (ed.). *Original Journals of
the Lewis and Clark Expedition, 1804-1806.*
Arno Press, 1969.

ACKNOWLEDGEMENTS

We would like to thank all the people who
helped in the preparation of this cookbook.
The following people tested recipes for us:

*Shelby Basset, Kaaren Black, Rich Bohn, Tim
Brennan, Jerry Brown, Lisa Disdero, Dianne
Duprez, Marie Finlay, Carolyn Glenn, Debby
Halliburton, Florence Hardcastle, Helen and
Merlyn Hobson, Theresa Holgate, Marie
Johnson, Irene Jue, Evelyn and Raymond
Main, Margaret and Manuel Main, Peter and
Maggie Marcus, Robin Milam, George Morgan,
Shirley and Bob Nichols, Kaye Norton, Rose
Preston, Frank Ross, Kathleen Sayce, Larry
Skinner, Valerie Smith, Jennice and Hal
Snow, Betty Synder, Bonnie Soule, Patty
Thomas, Carol Weigardt, Fred and Eva
Werkman, Melinda Williams, Karen Winn.*

LIST OF REGIONAL SKETCHES

PHOTO LOCATIONS

INDEX

Tarragon
  Chicken and Scallops with
  Tarragon 94
Tartar Sauce 171
  Halibut du Chef 82
Tequila
  Scallops Nectarine 40
Teriyaki Sauce 91
  Sake Scallops 91
Tomato Sauce 172
Tournedos with Green
  Peppercorns 103
Triple Sec
  Scallops Nectarine 40

Veal with Pine Nuts 102
Vinaigrette 180
  Mediterranean Salad 62
  Zucchini Cod Salad 60

Walnut oil
  Vinaigrette 180

Walnuts
  Butterhorns 120
  Cranberry Chicken Salad 59
  Date Nut Bread 118
  Honey Bran Muffins 123
  Old Fashioned Bread
  Pudding 147
Watercress
  Smoked Salmon Pate 32
  Watercress Sauce 169
Wheat Germ Muffins 122
Whitefish
  Bouillabaisse 54
White Satin Tart ·158
Wild Blackberry Cheese
Tart 154

Zucchini
  Sauteed Zucchini Milam 63
  Zucchini Cod Salad 60